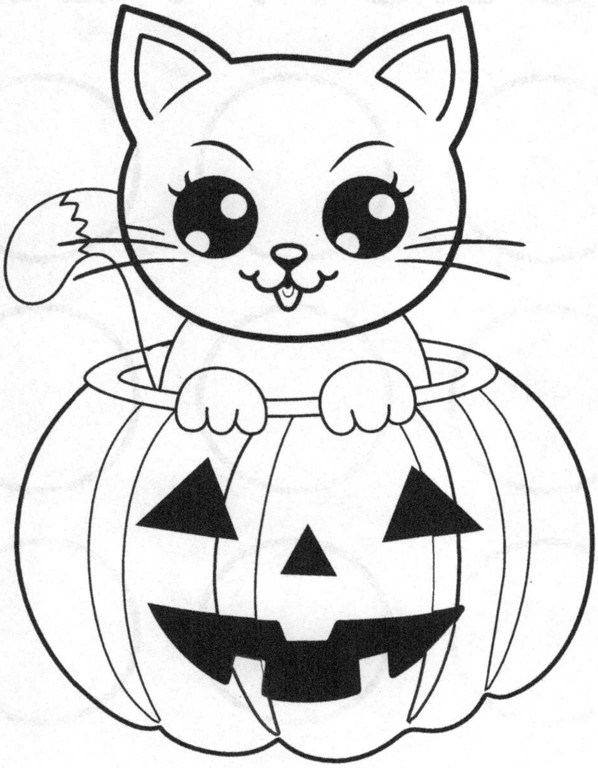

THIS BOOK BELONGS TO

____

____

COLOR TEST

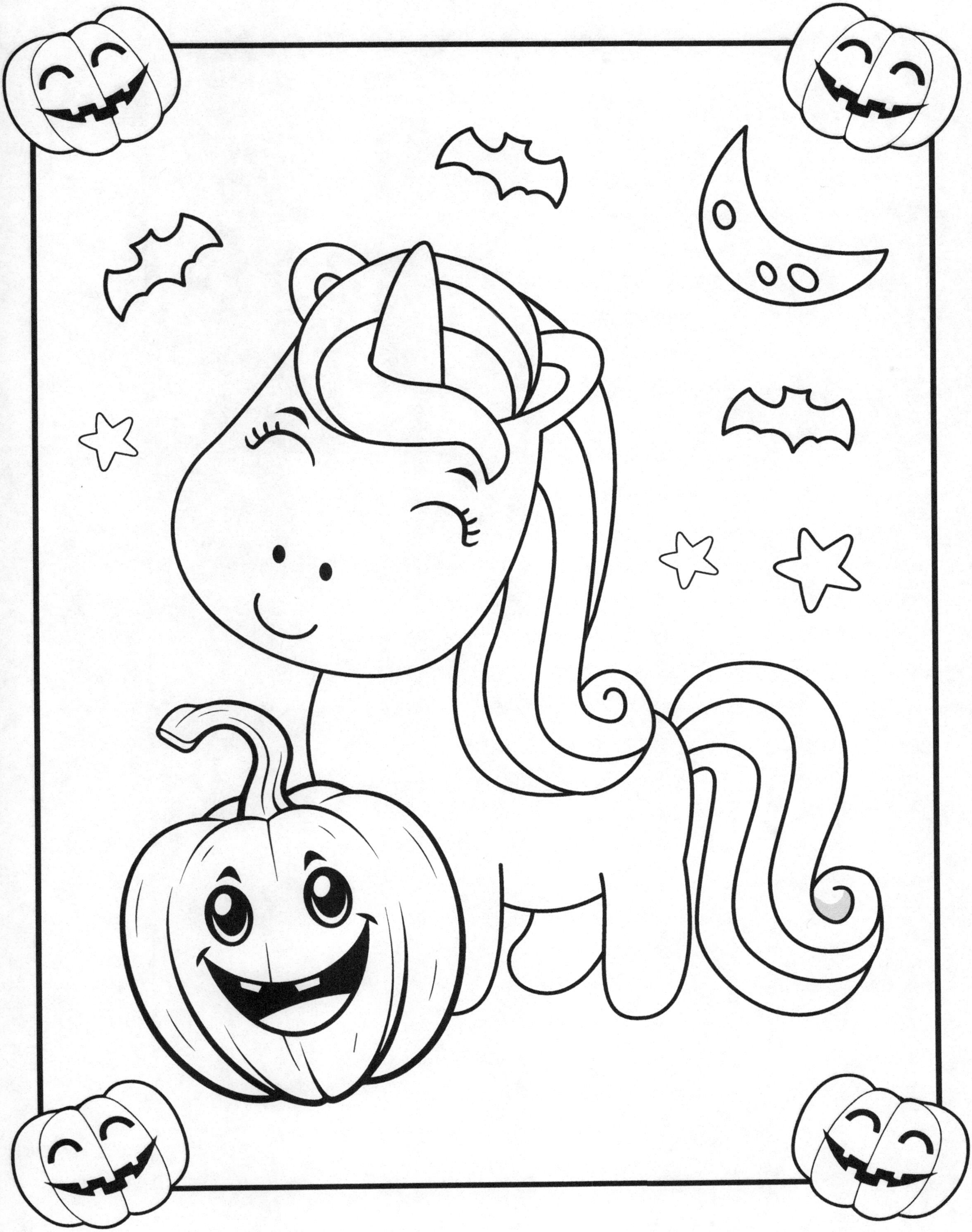

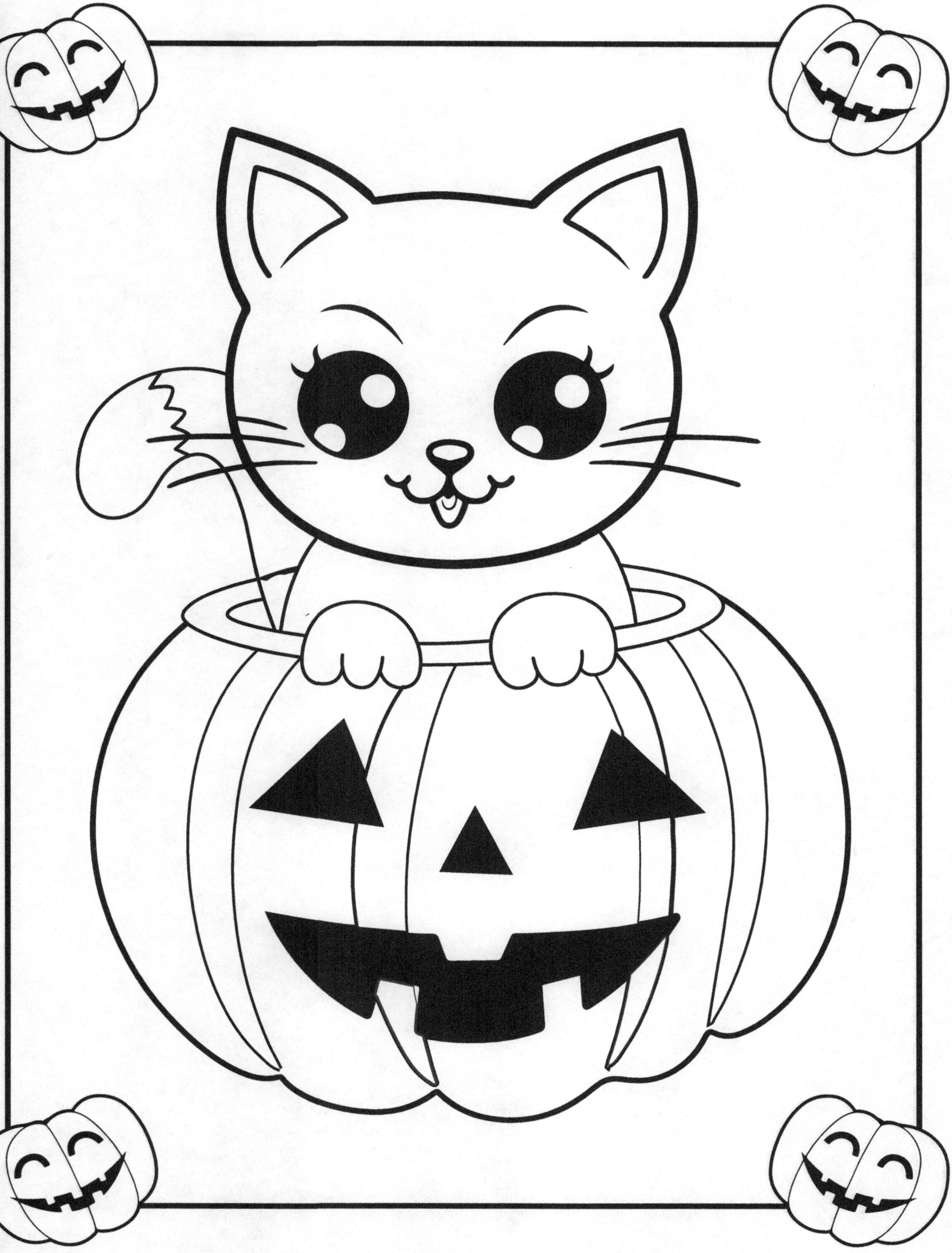

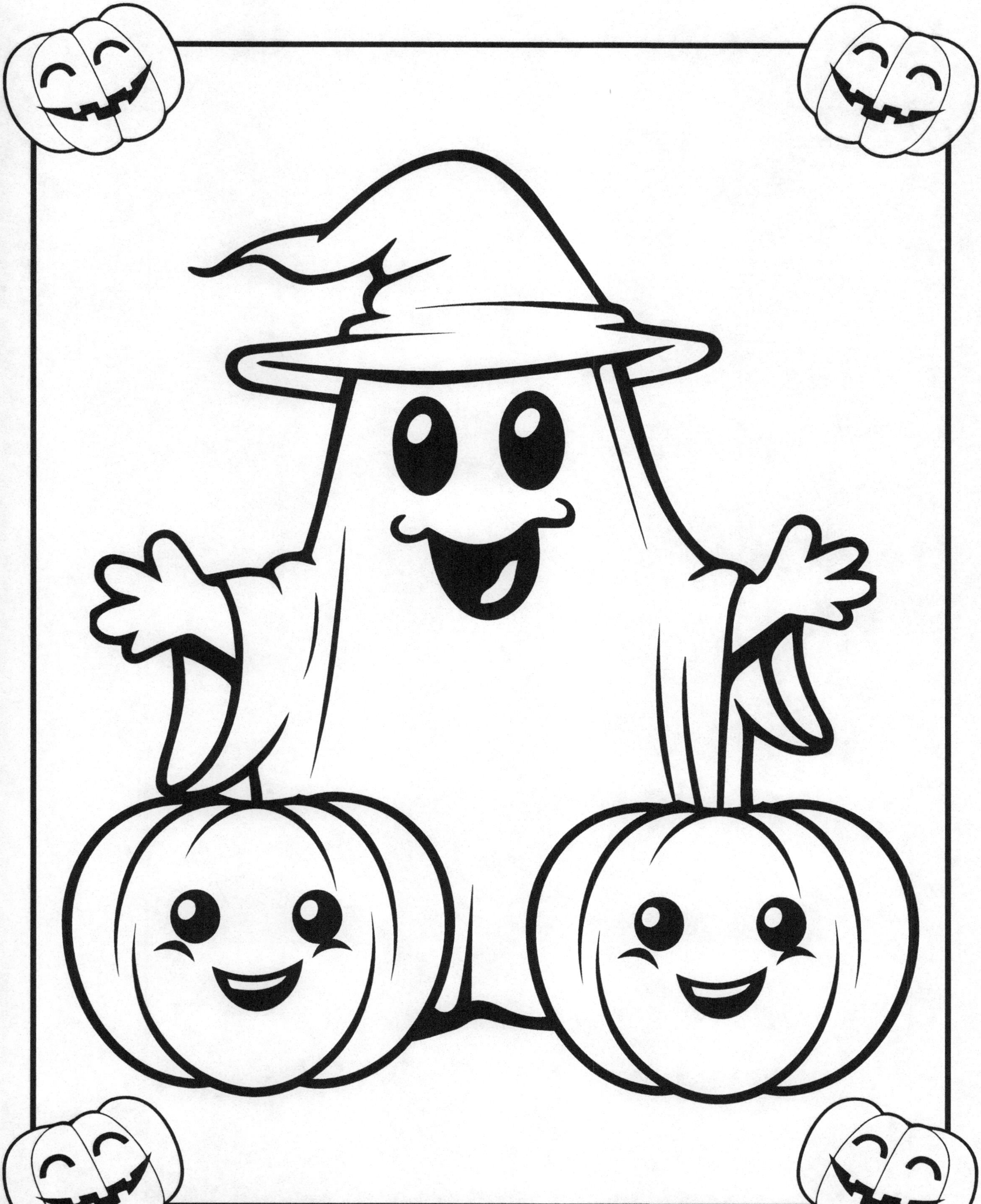

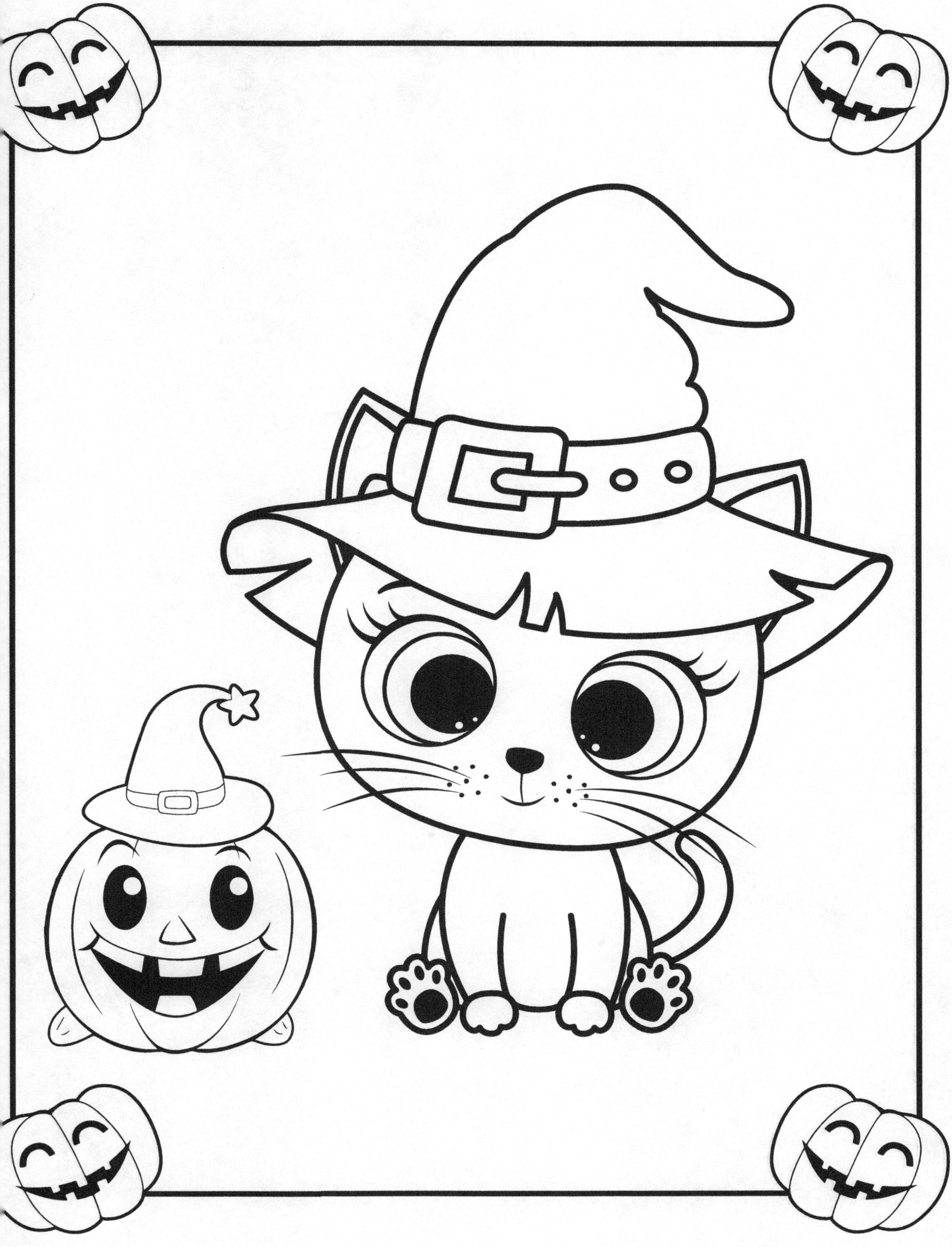

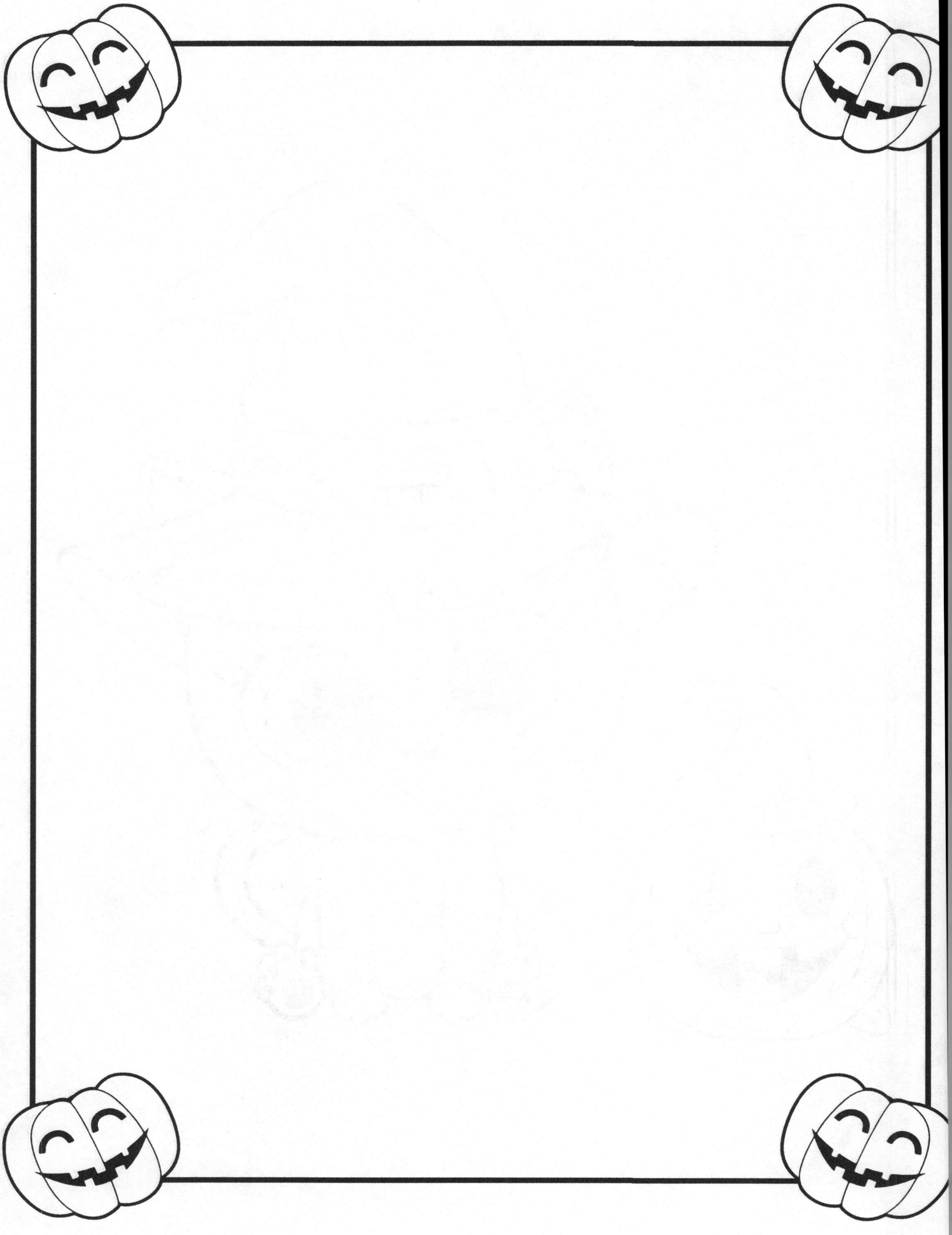

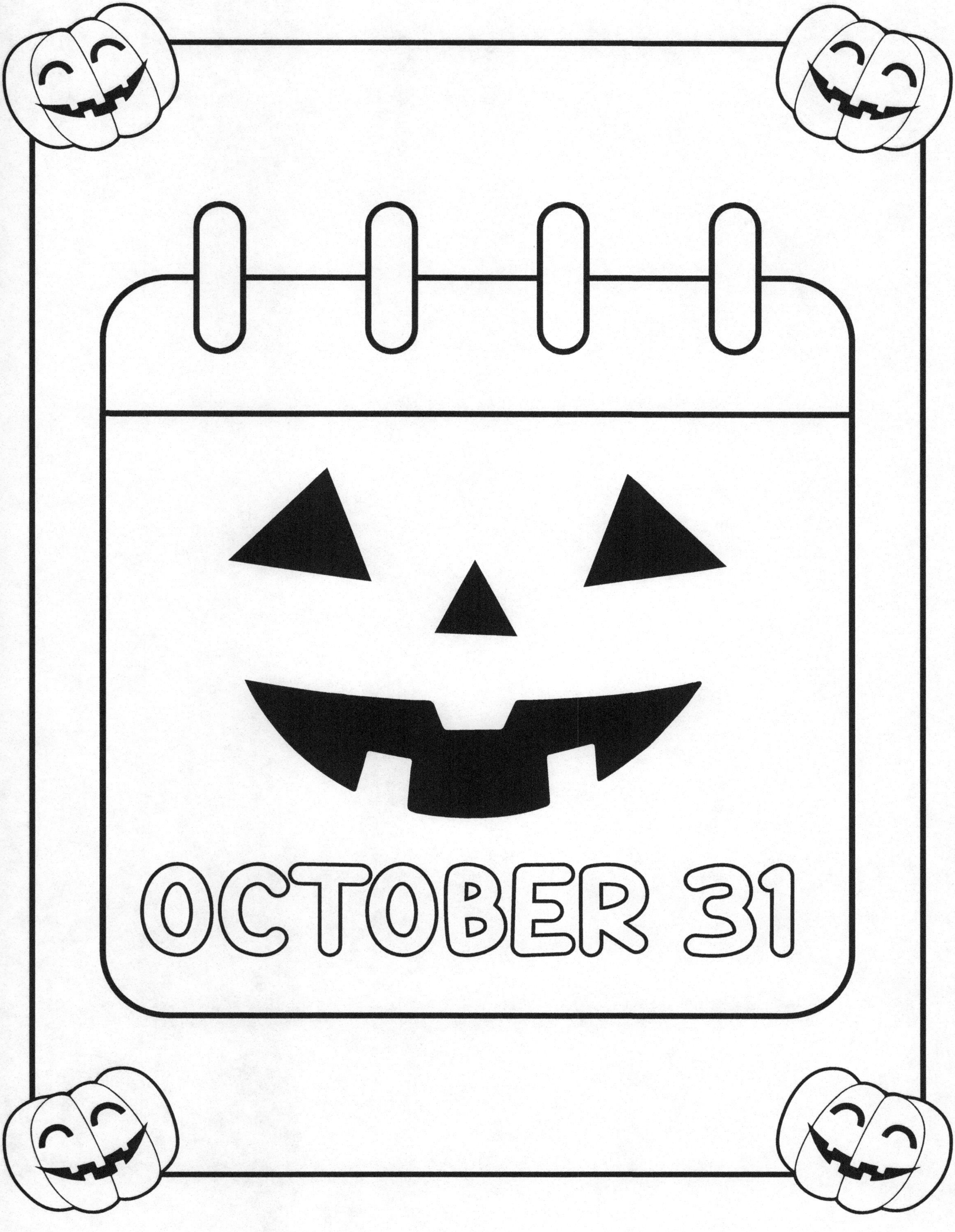
OCTOBER 31

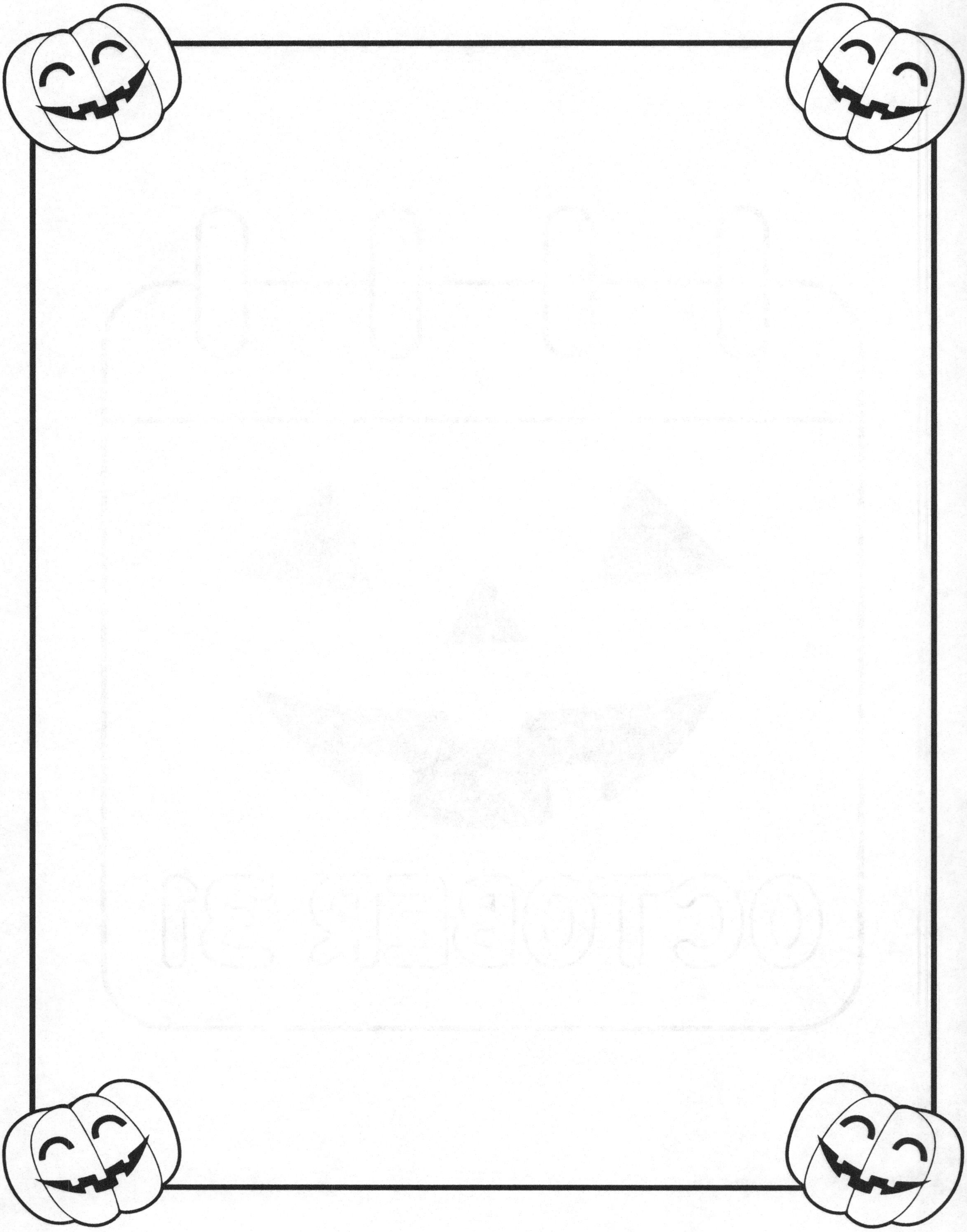

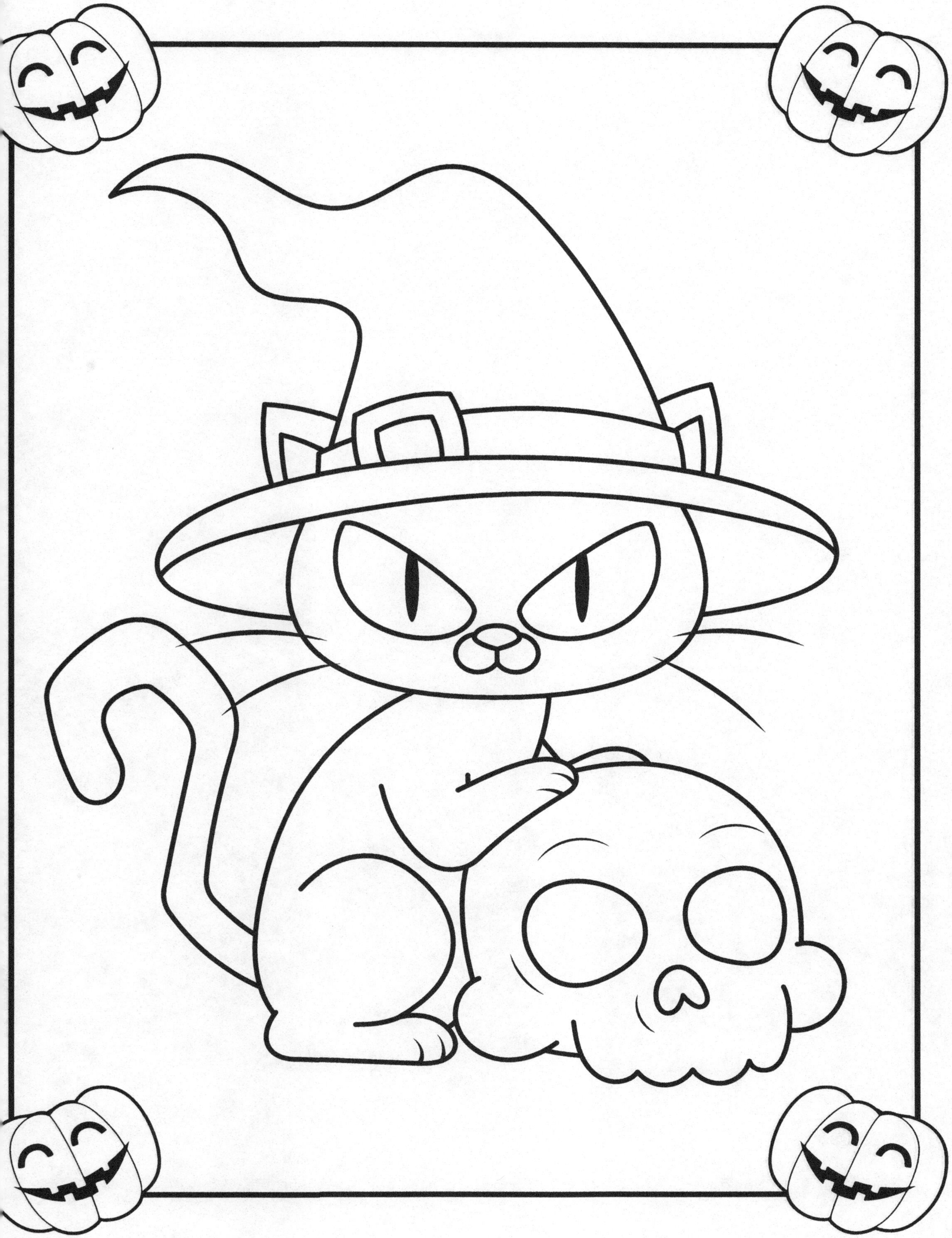

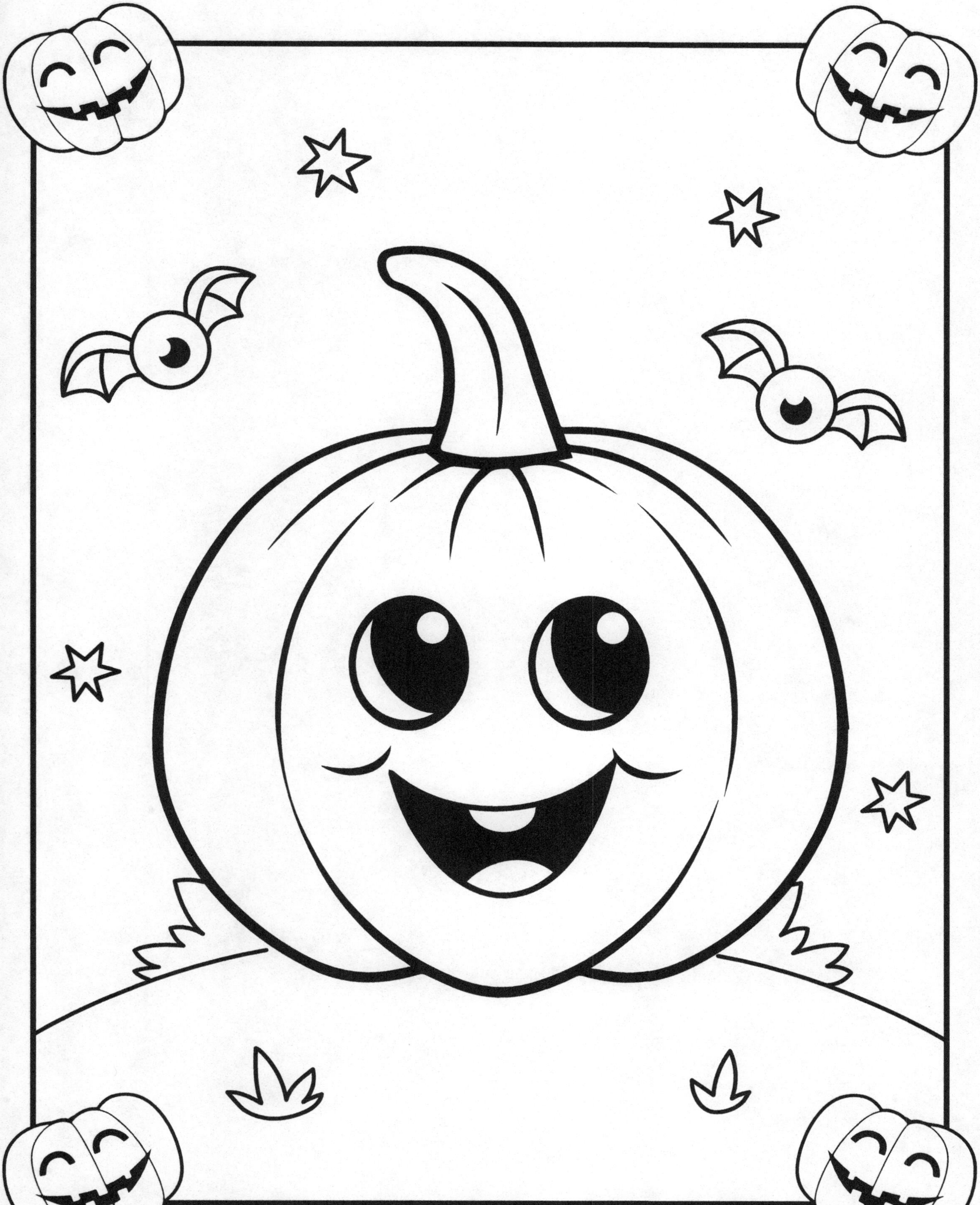

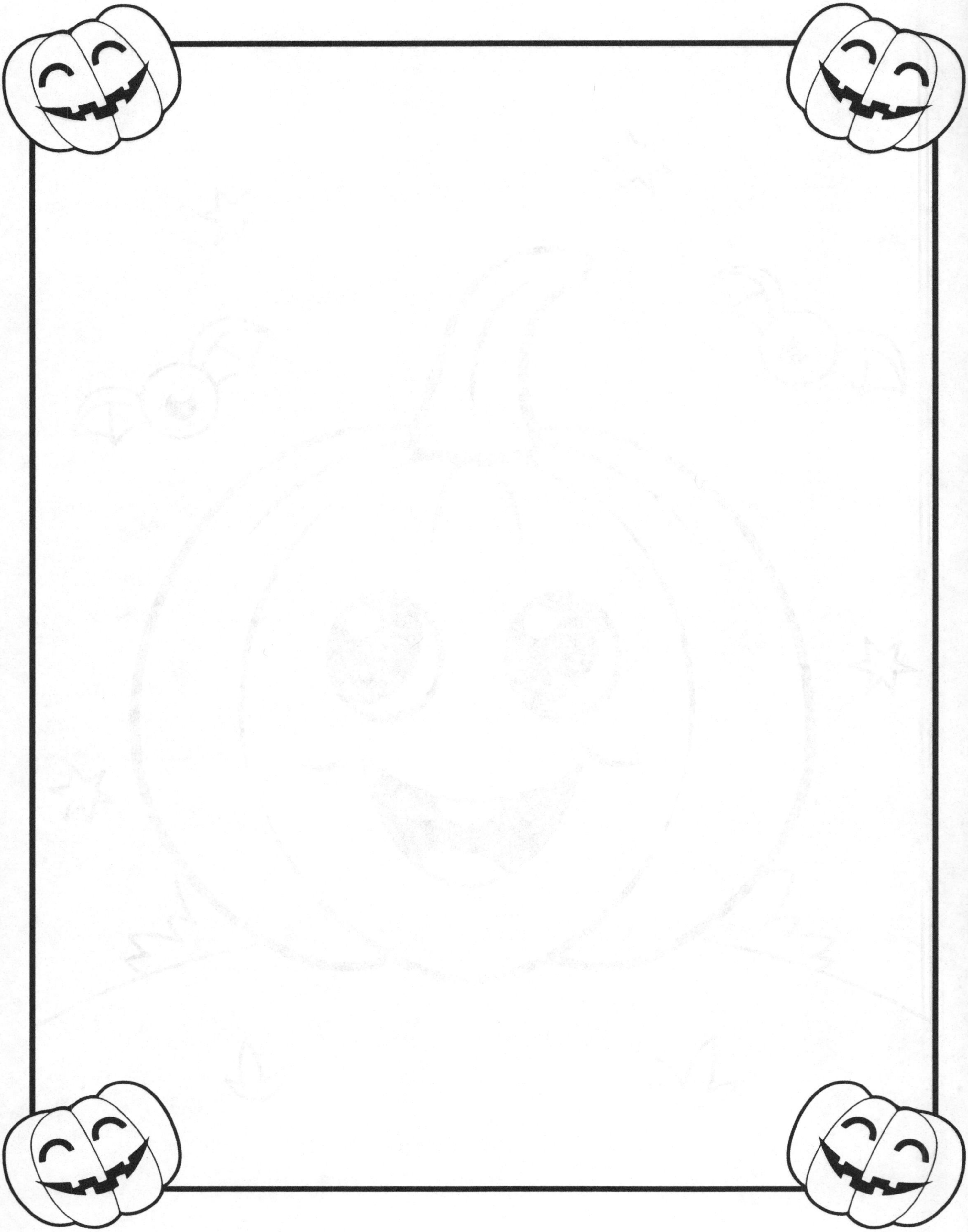

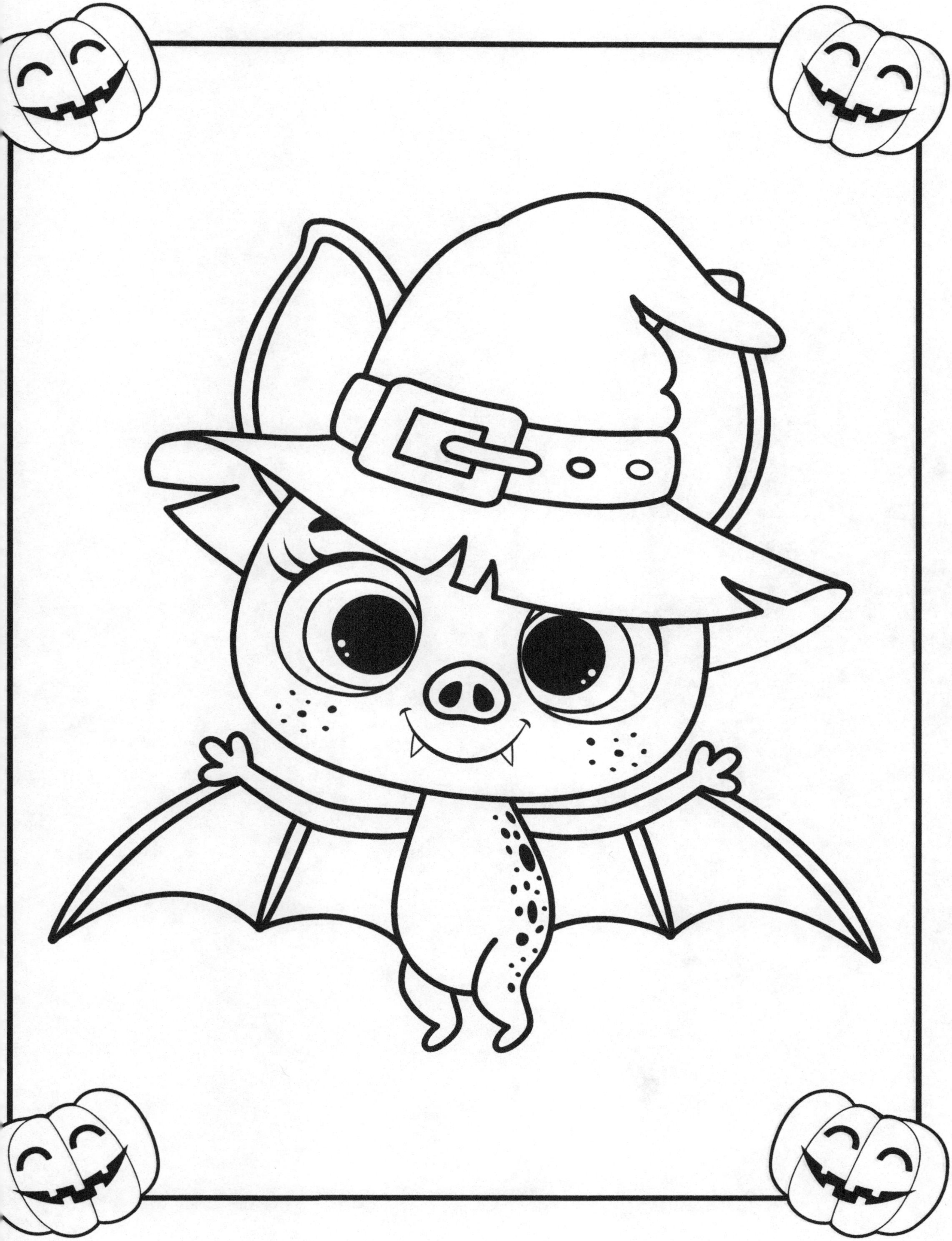

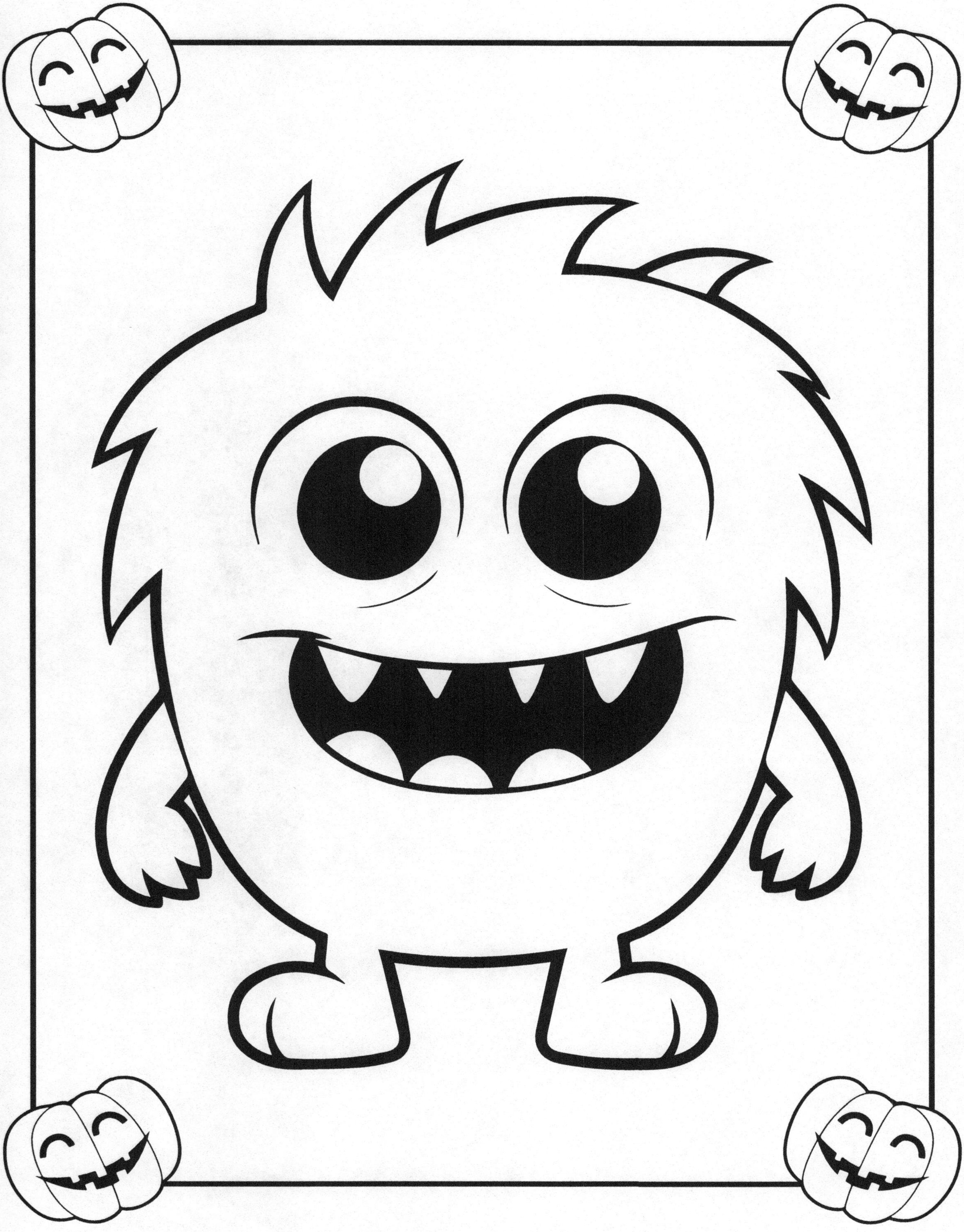

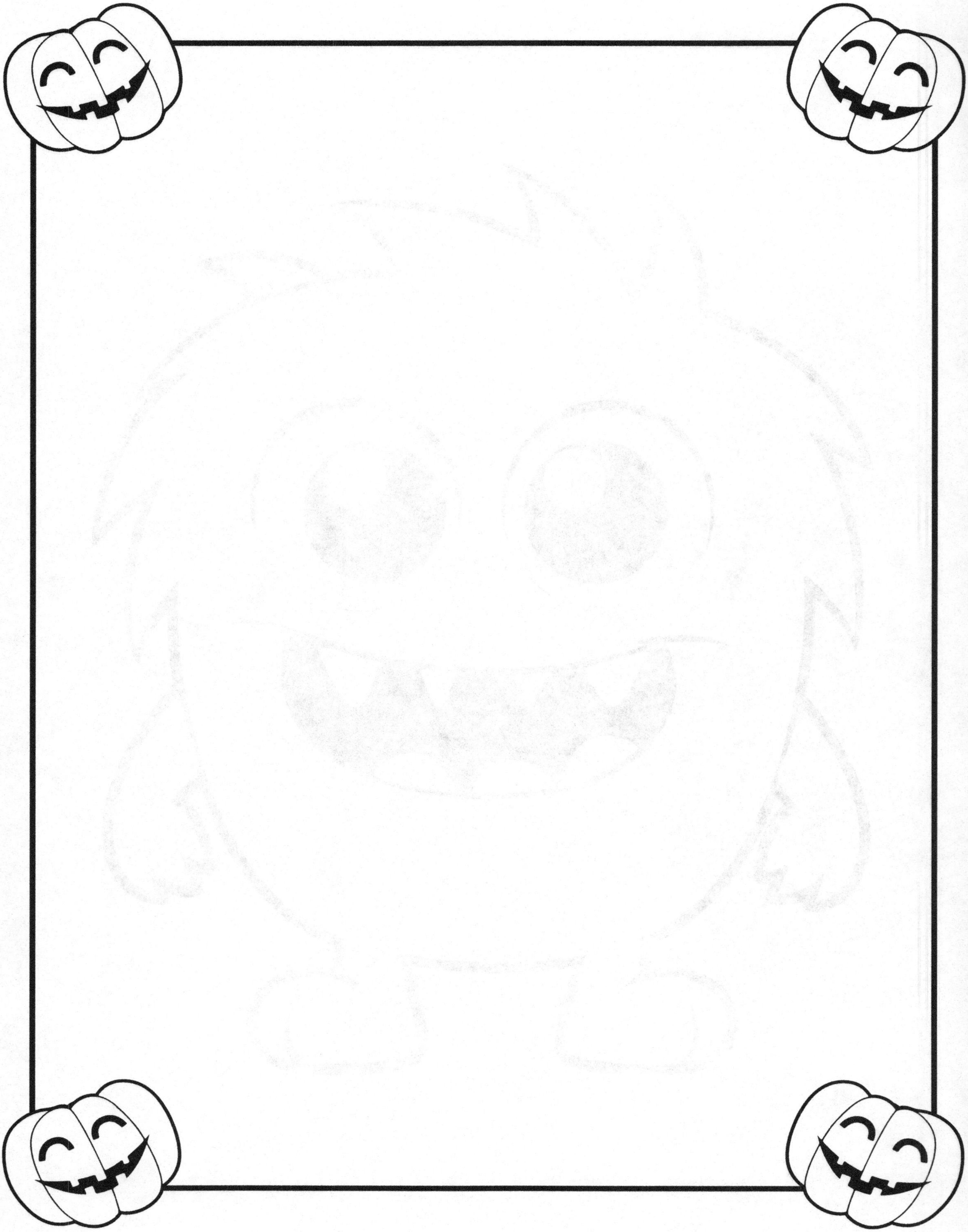

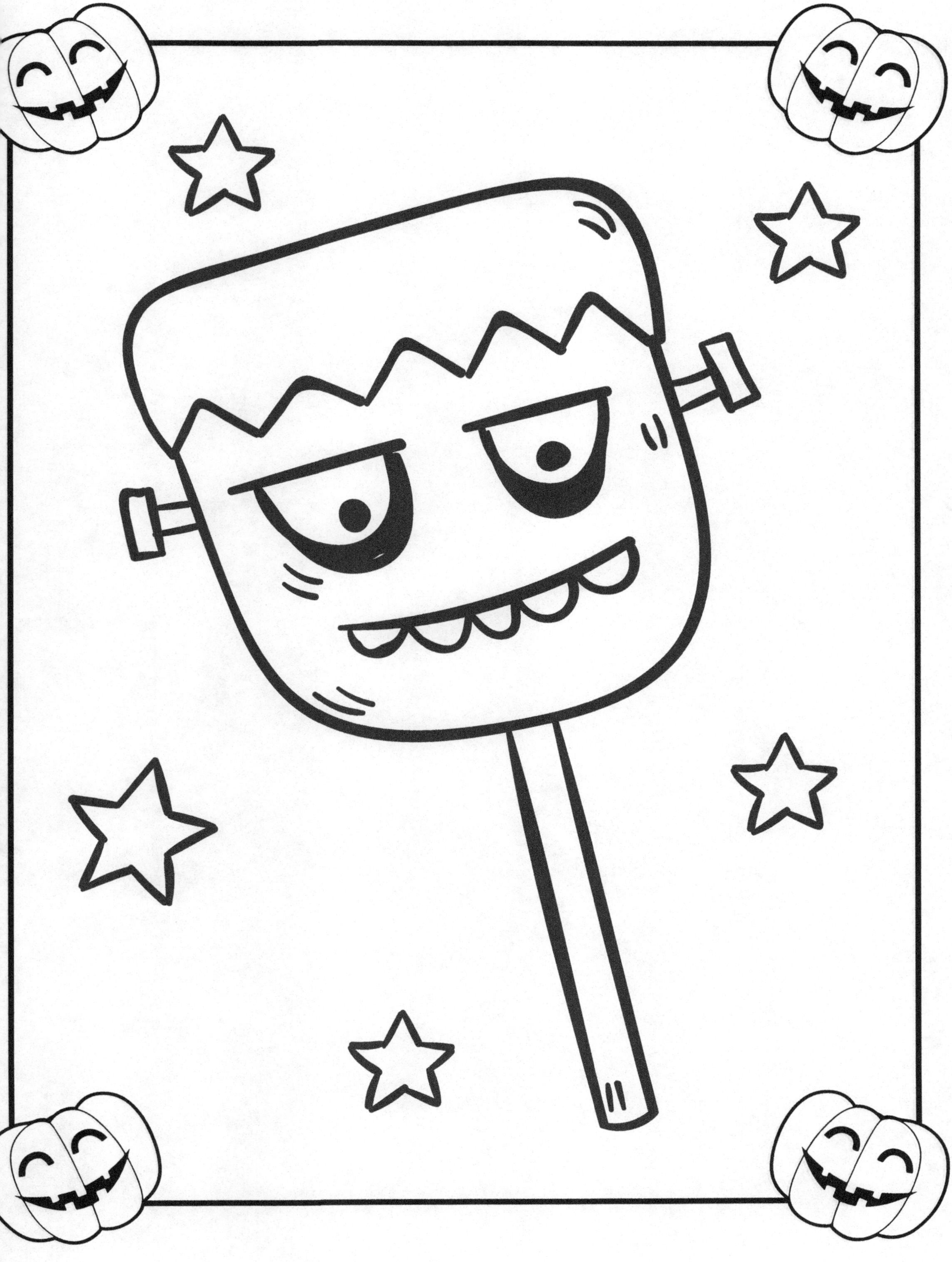

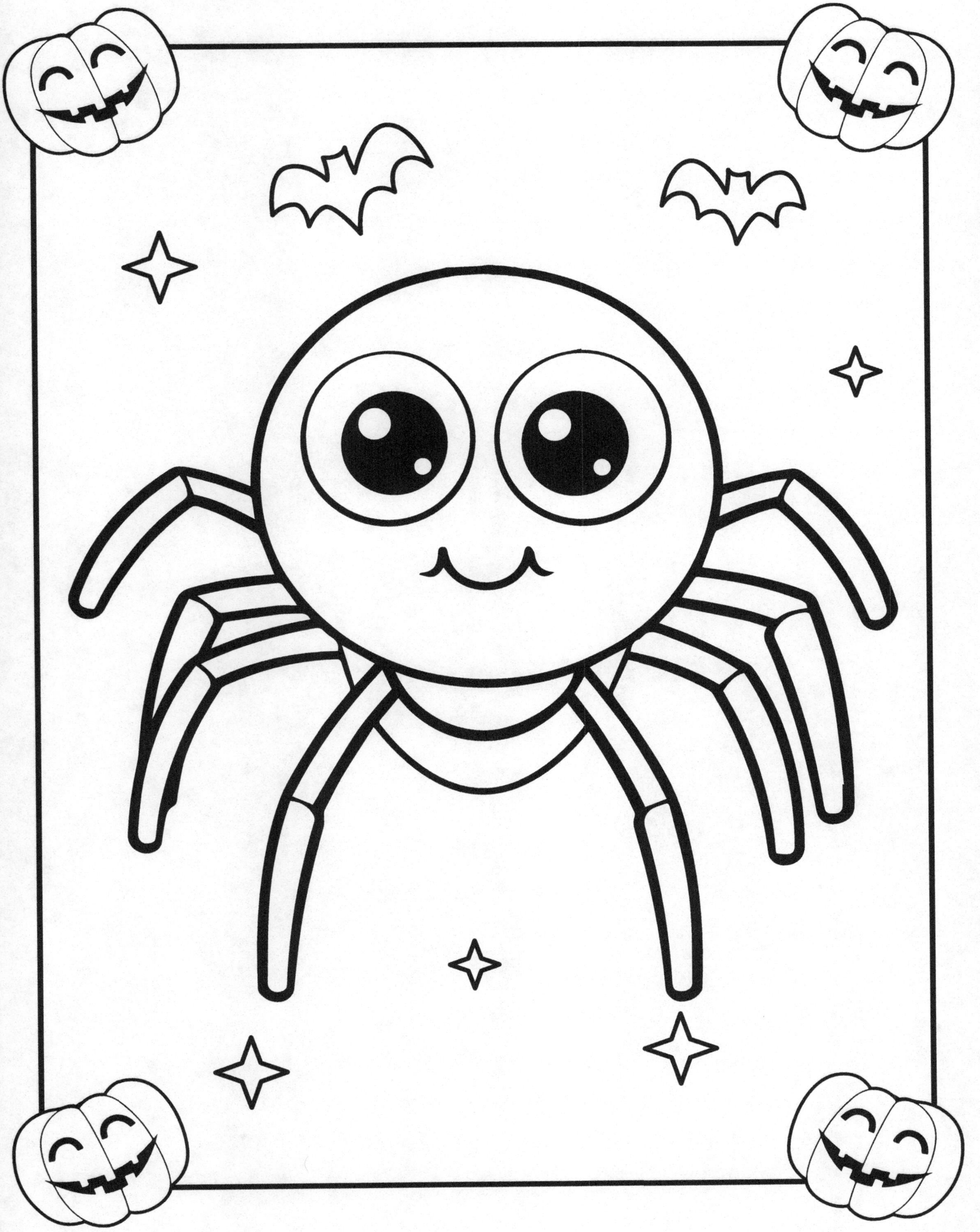

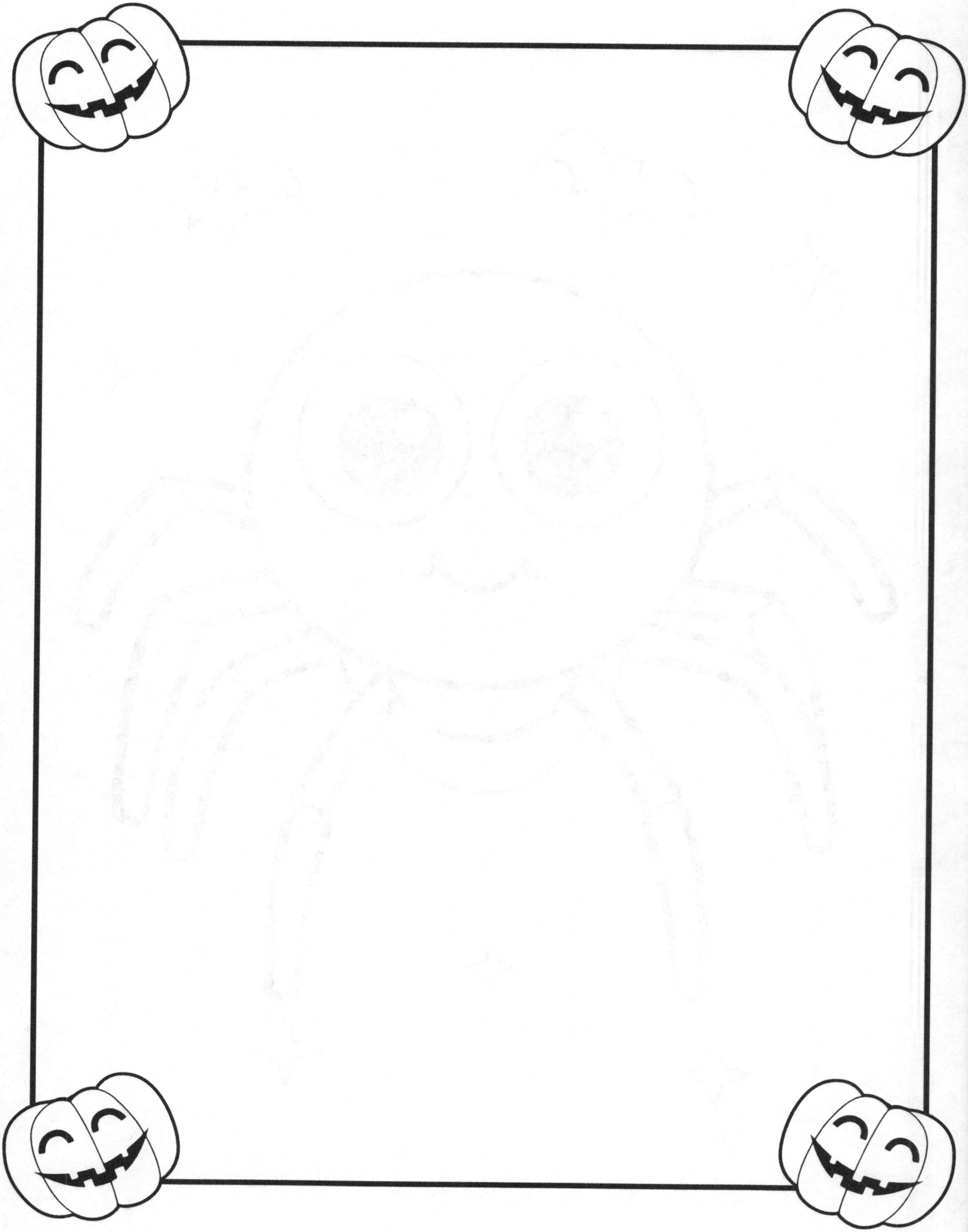

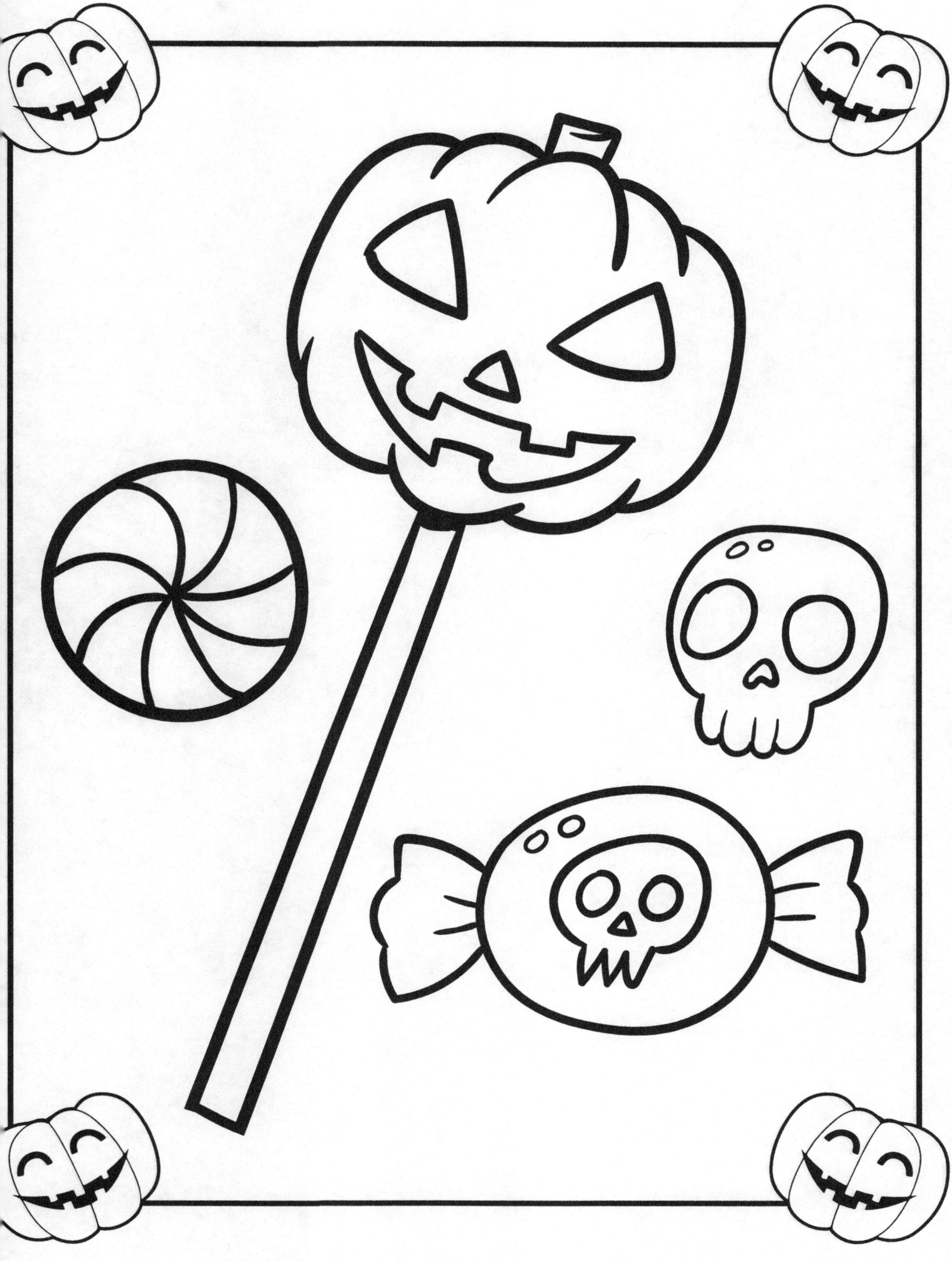

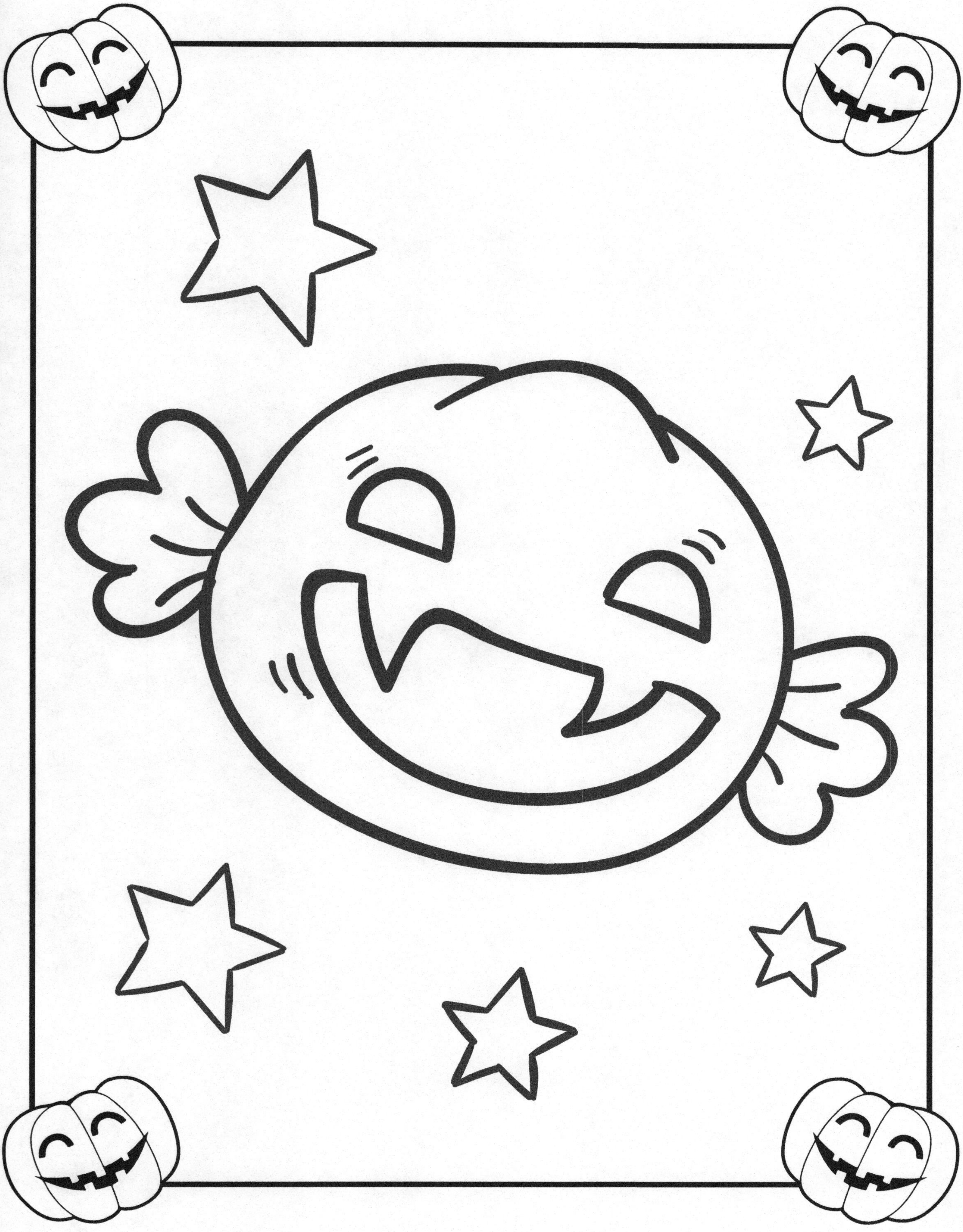

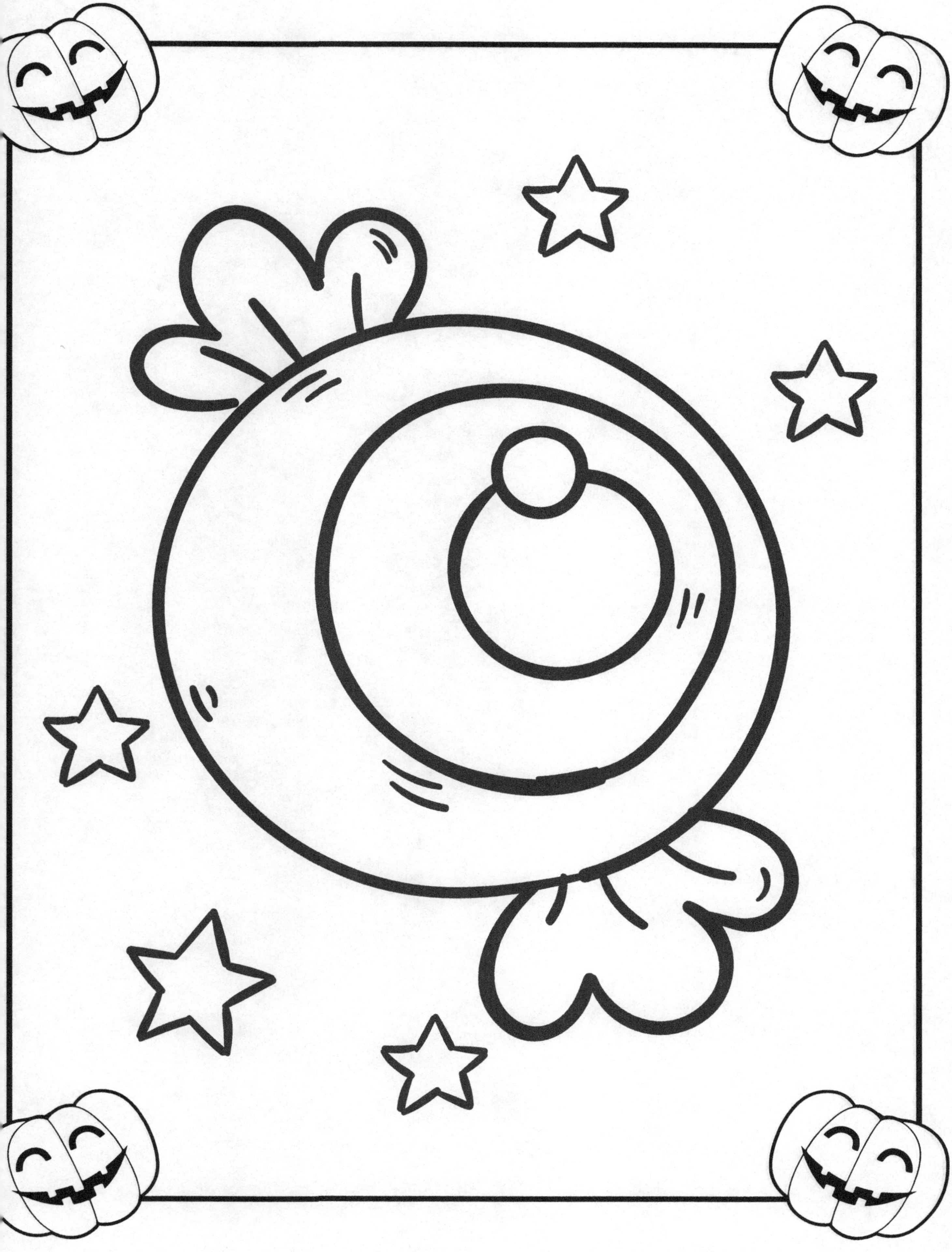

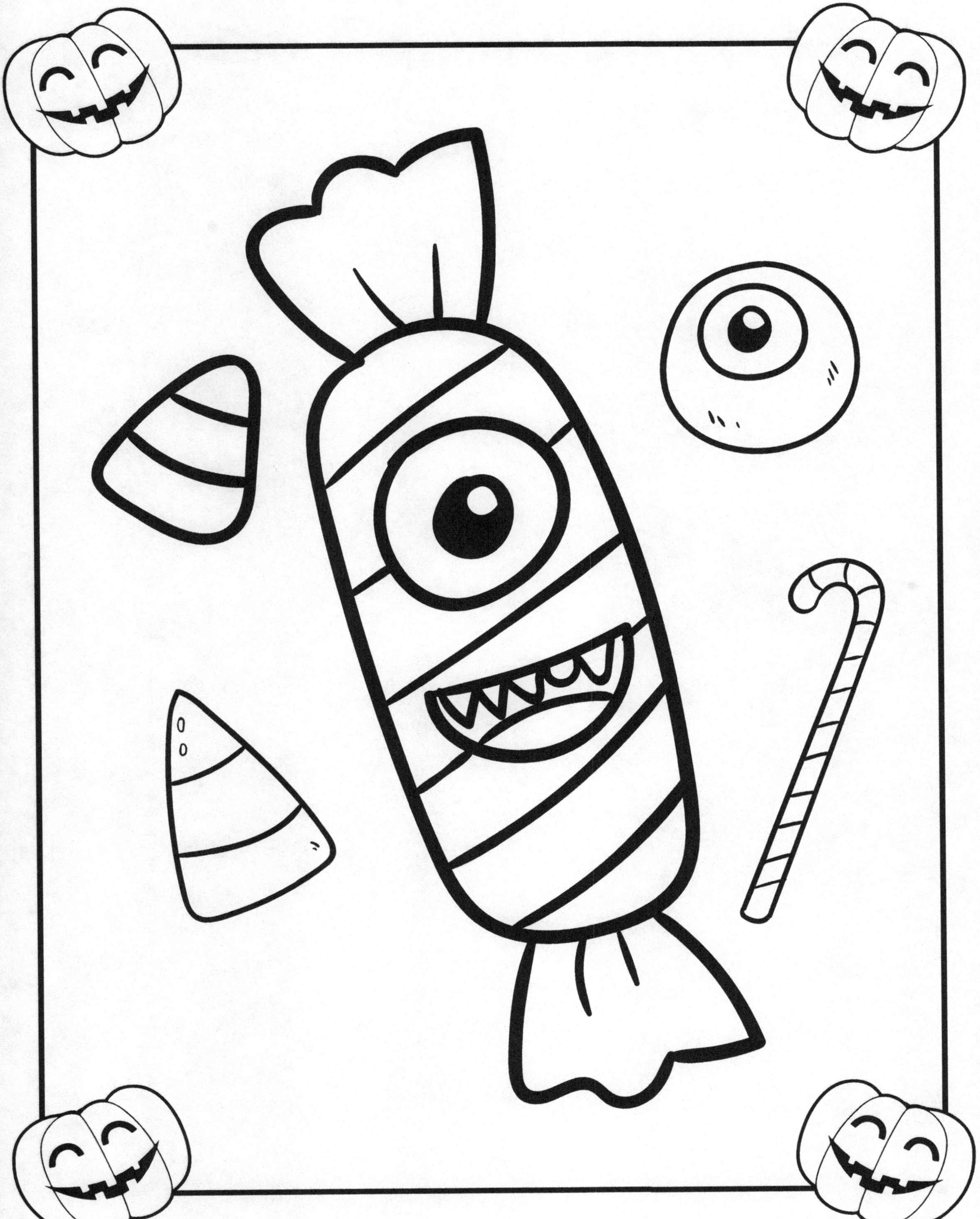

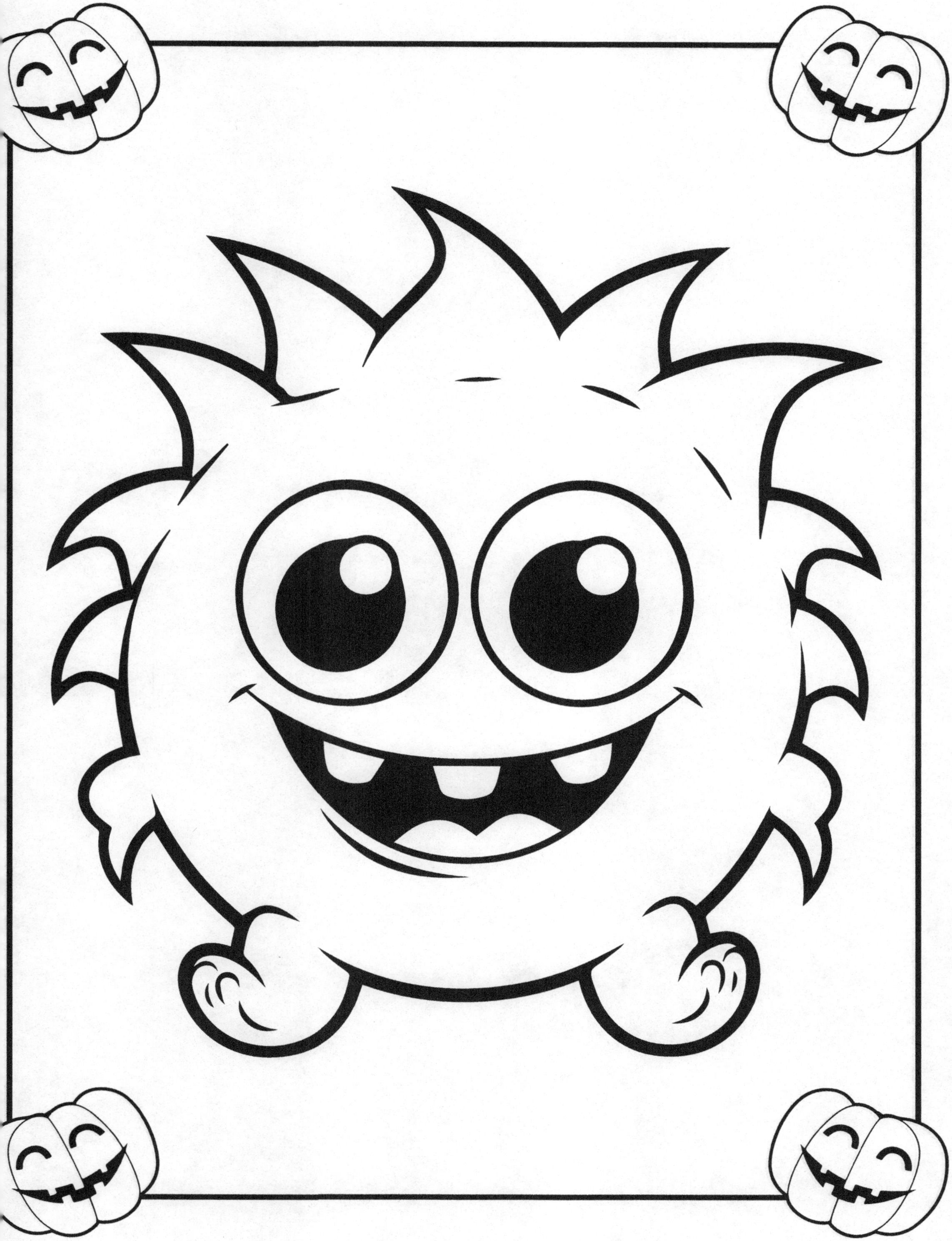

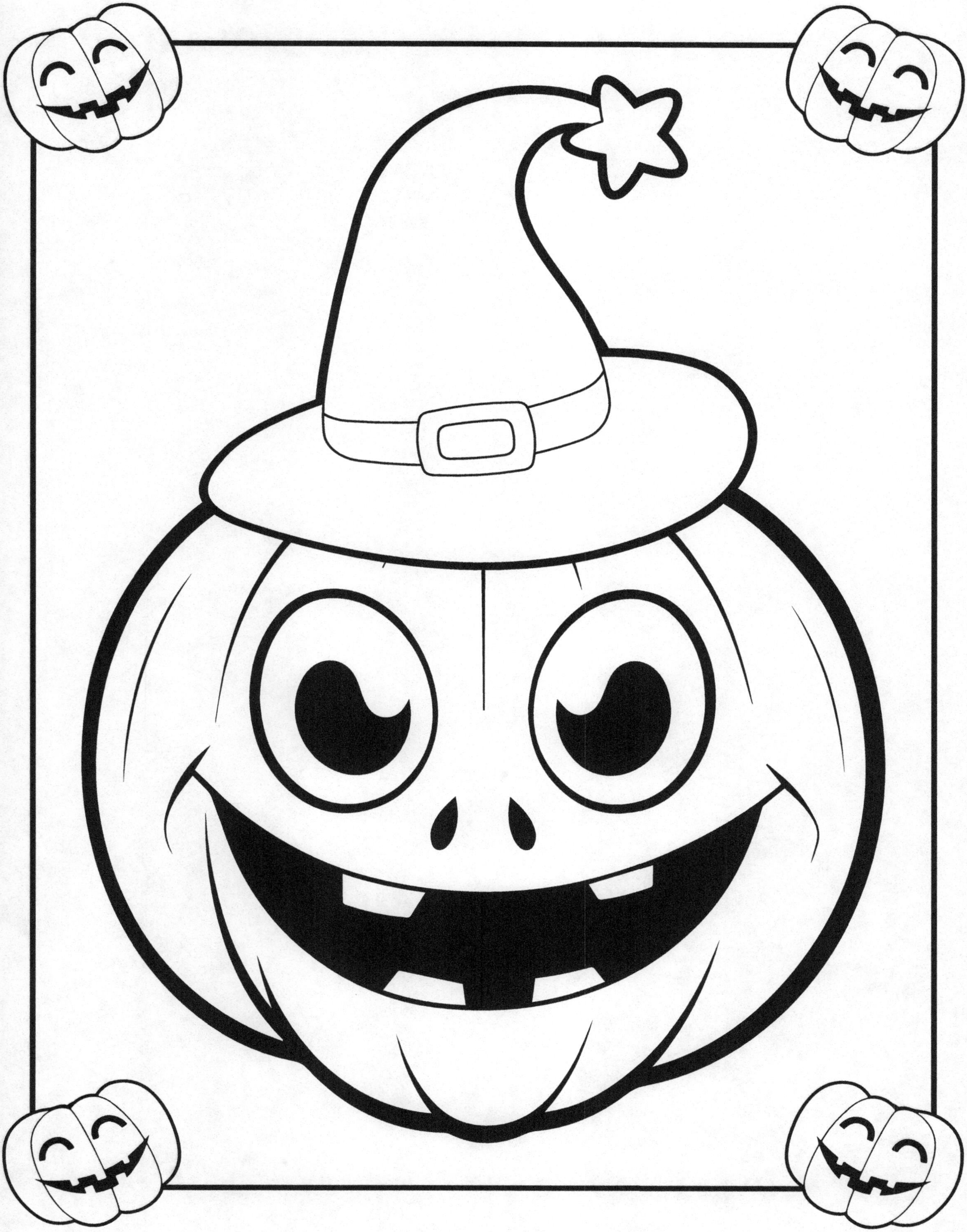

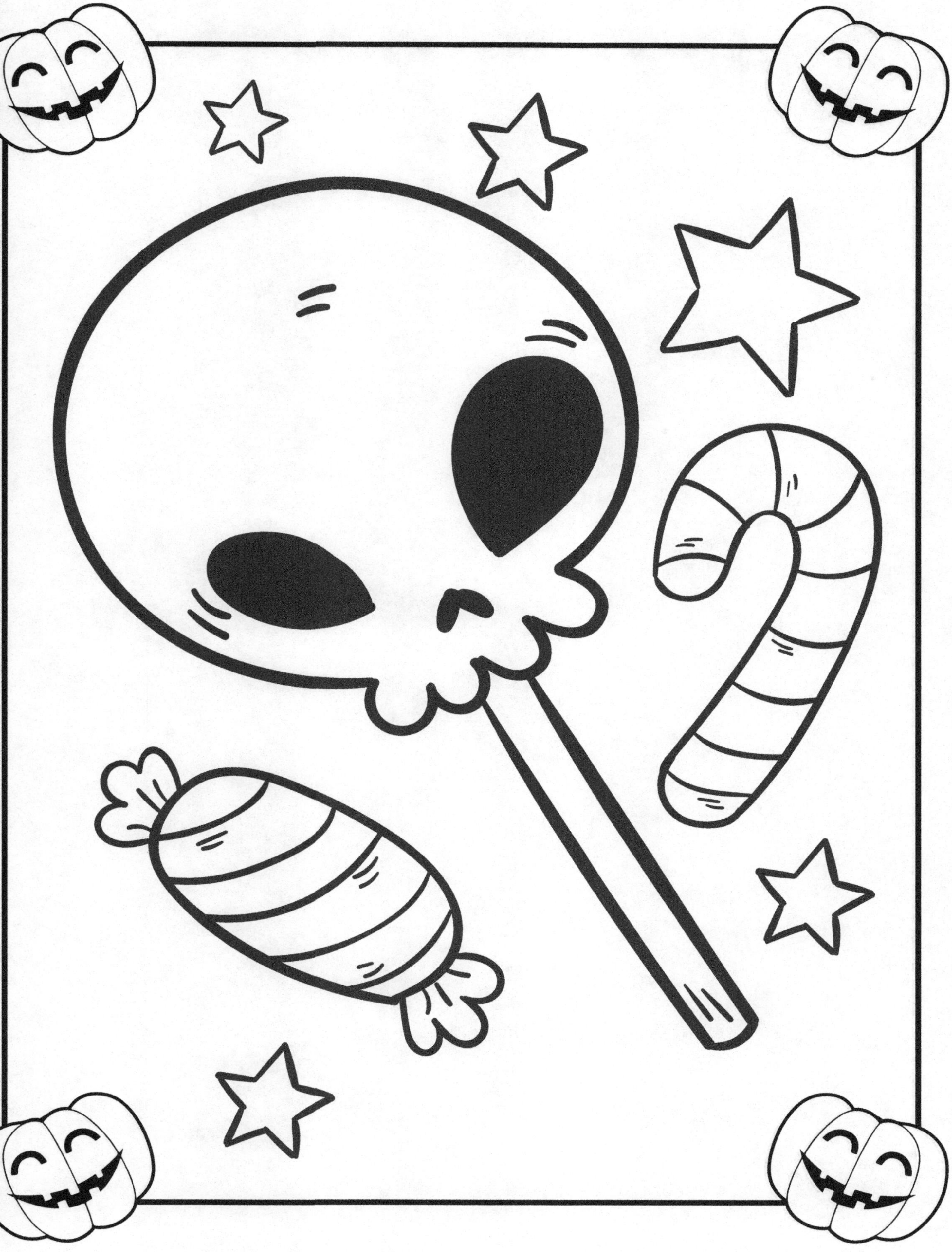

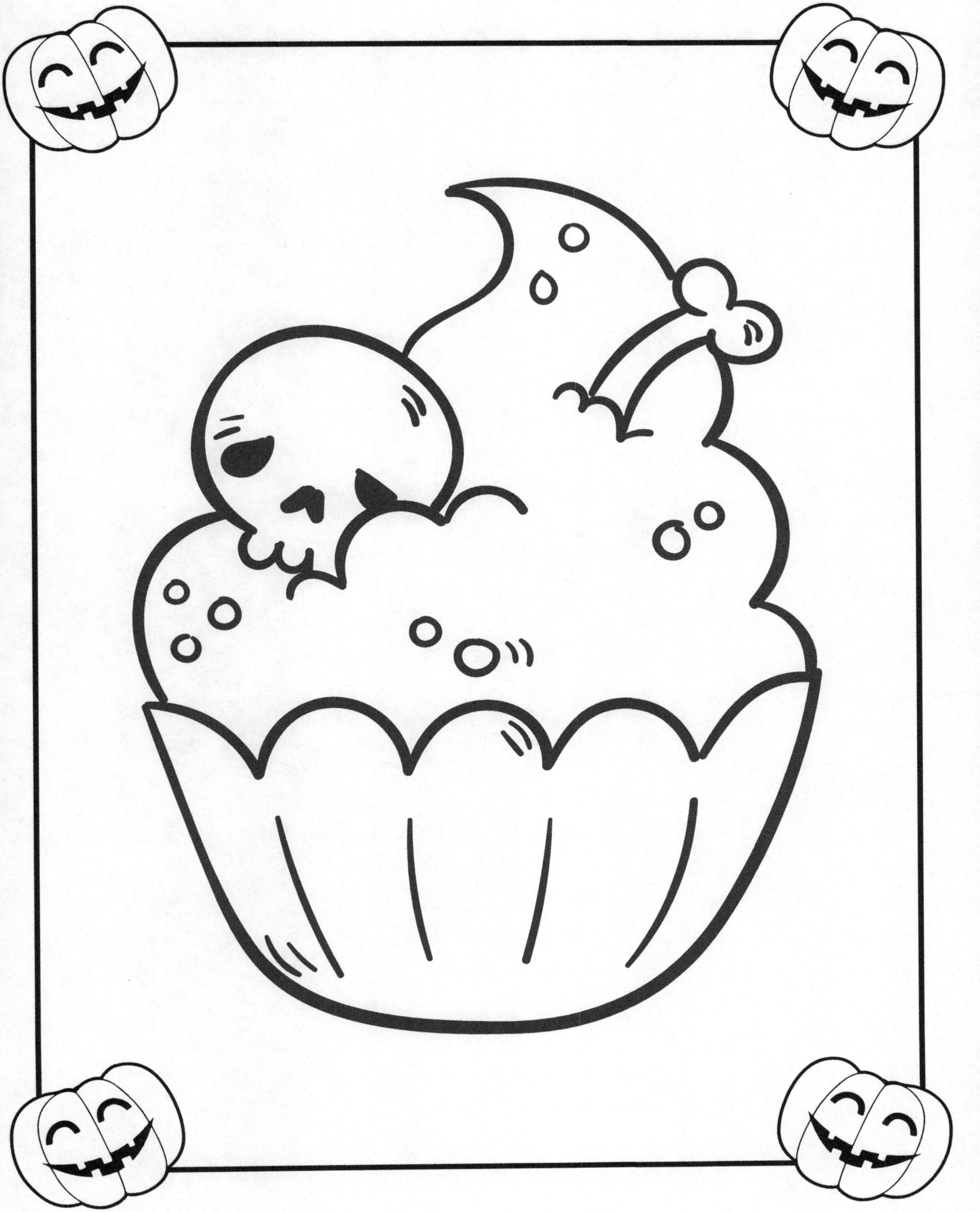

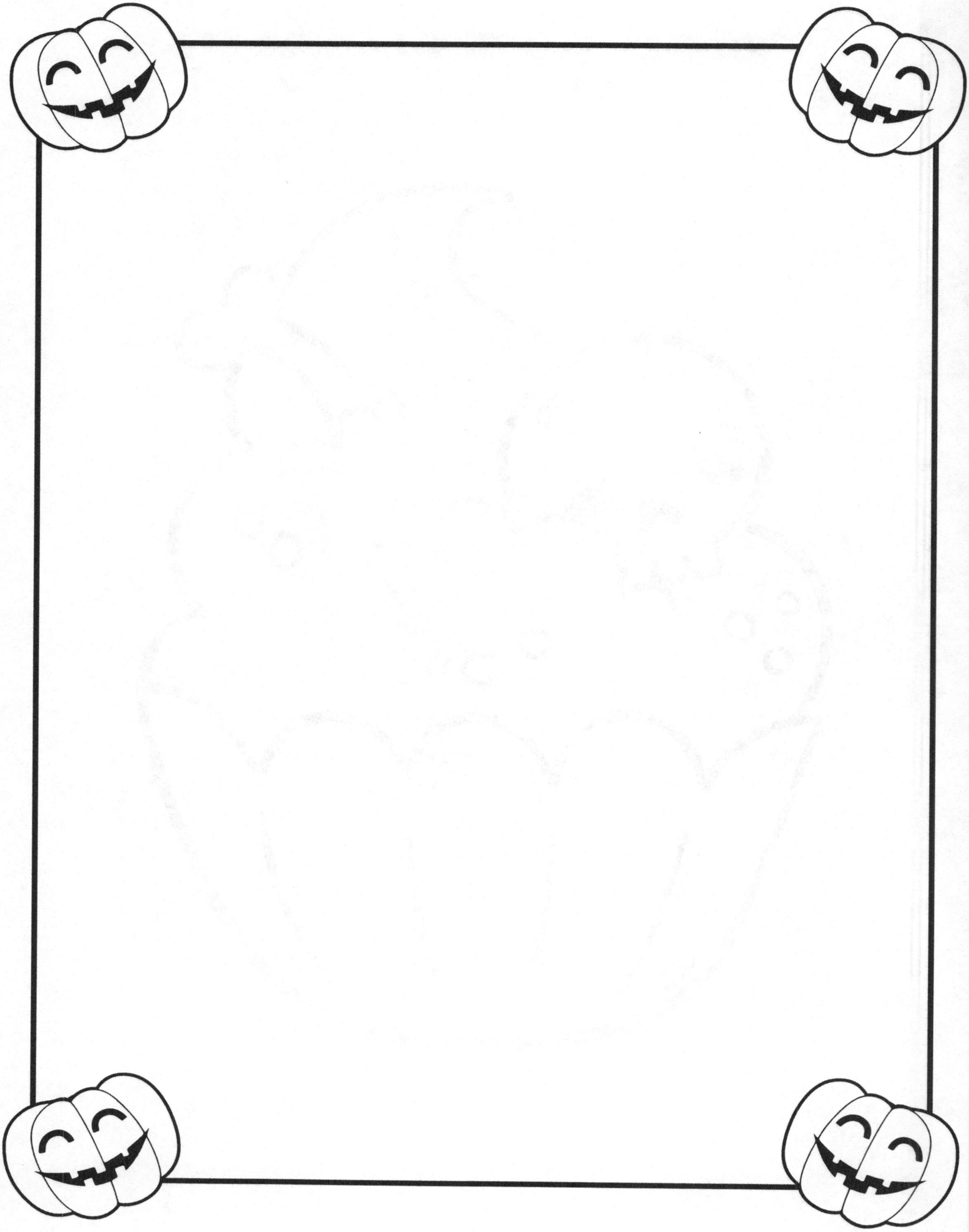

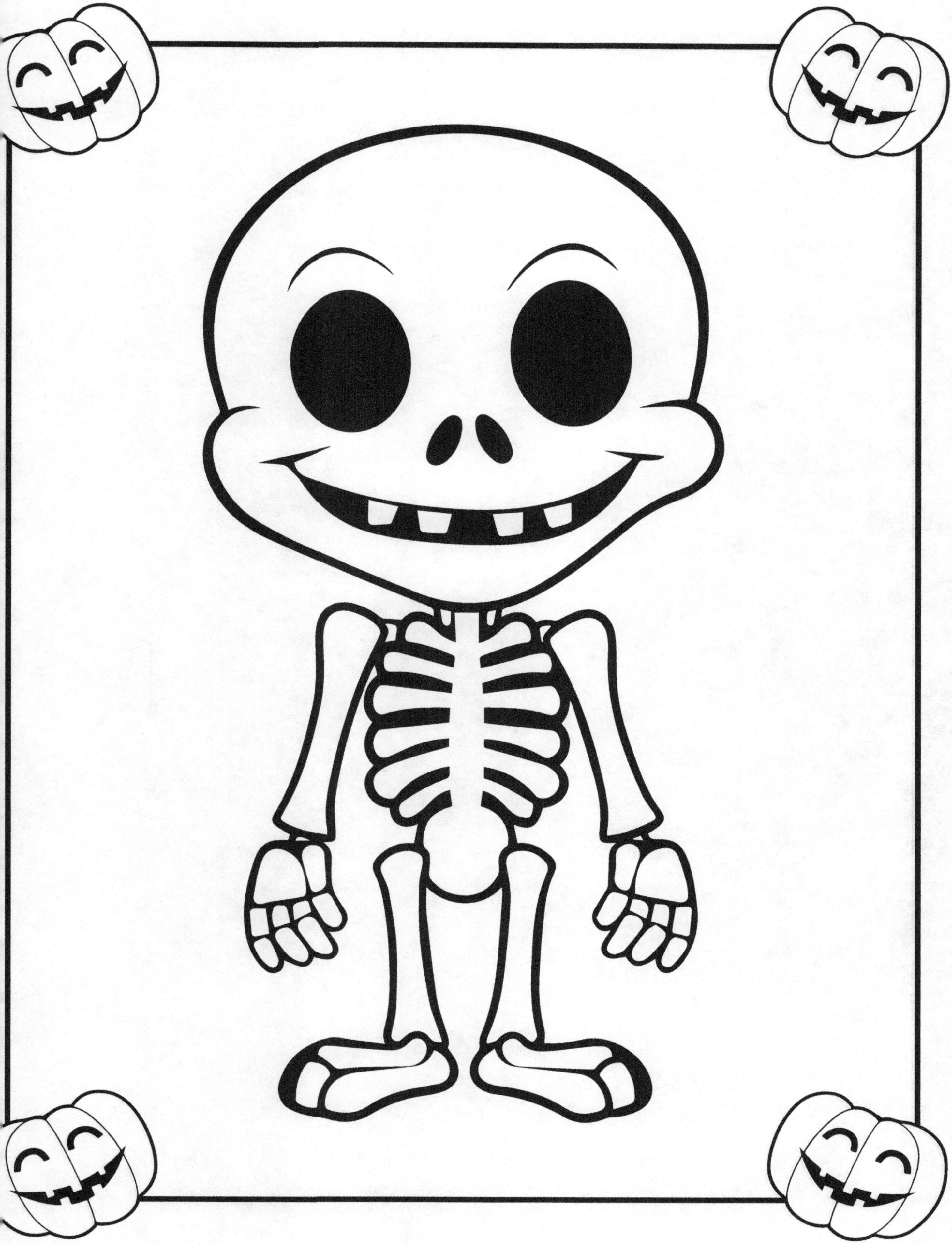

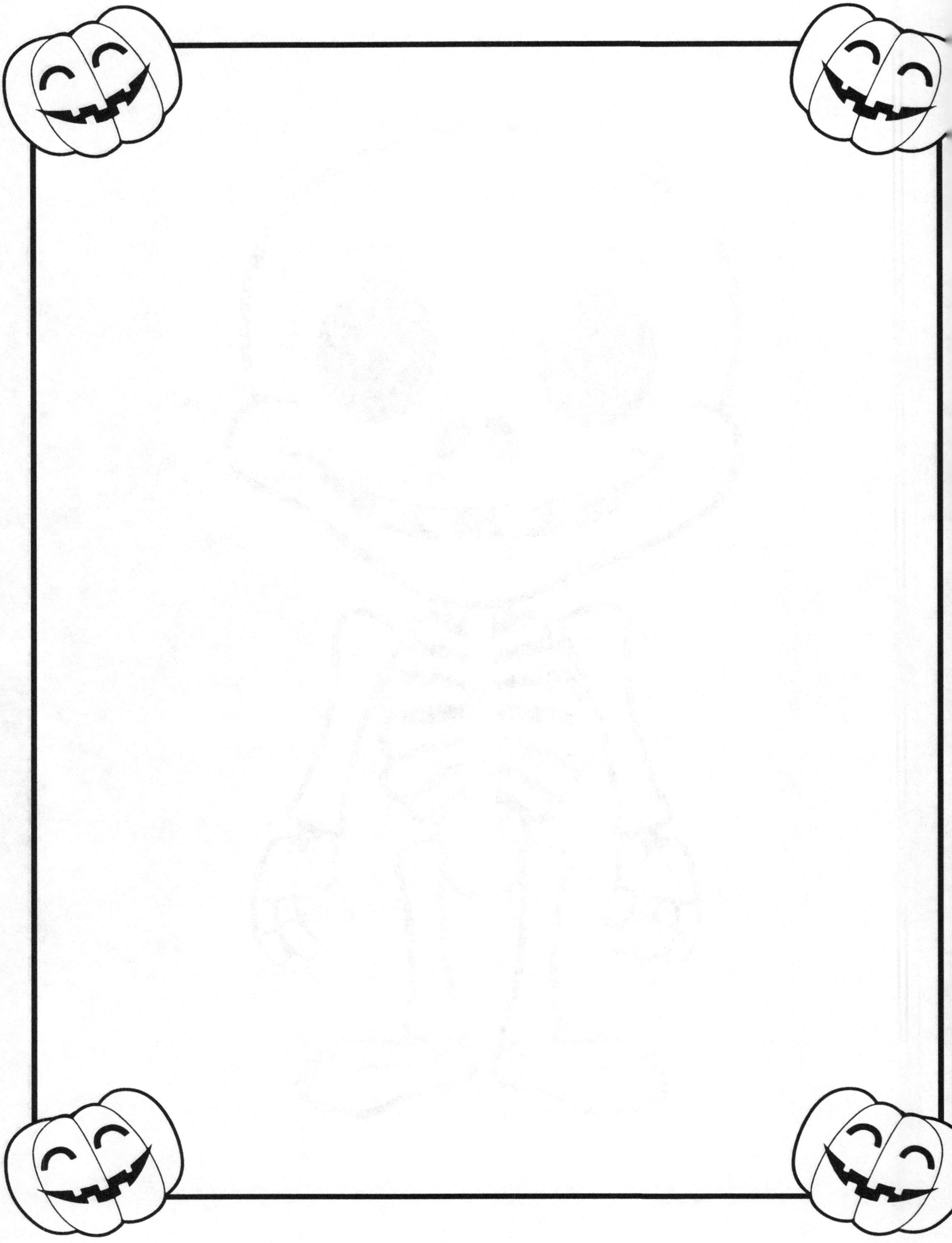

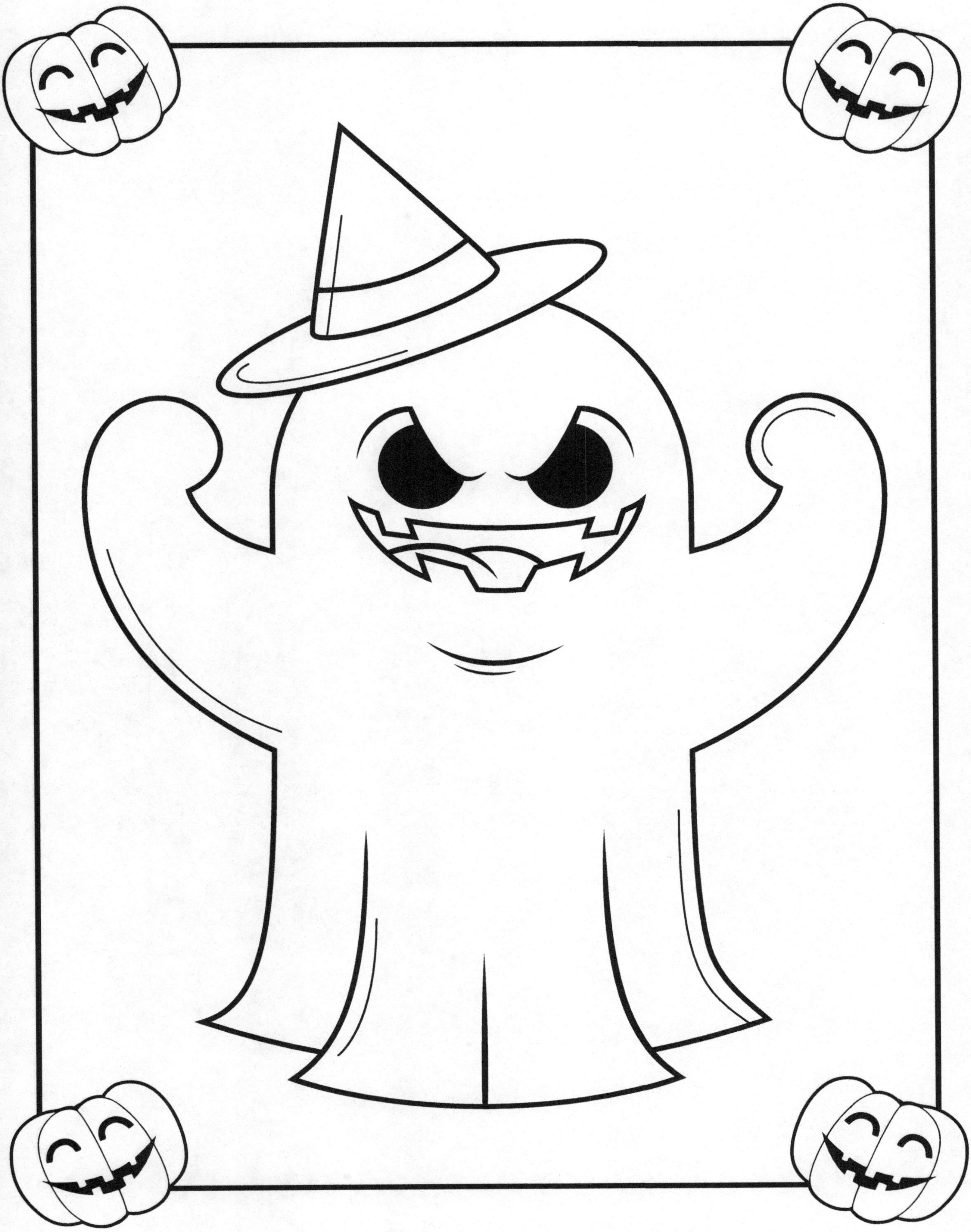

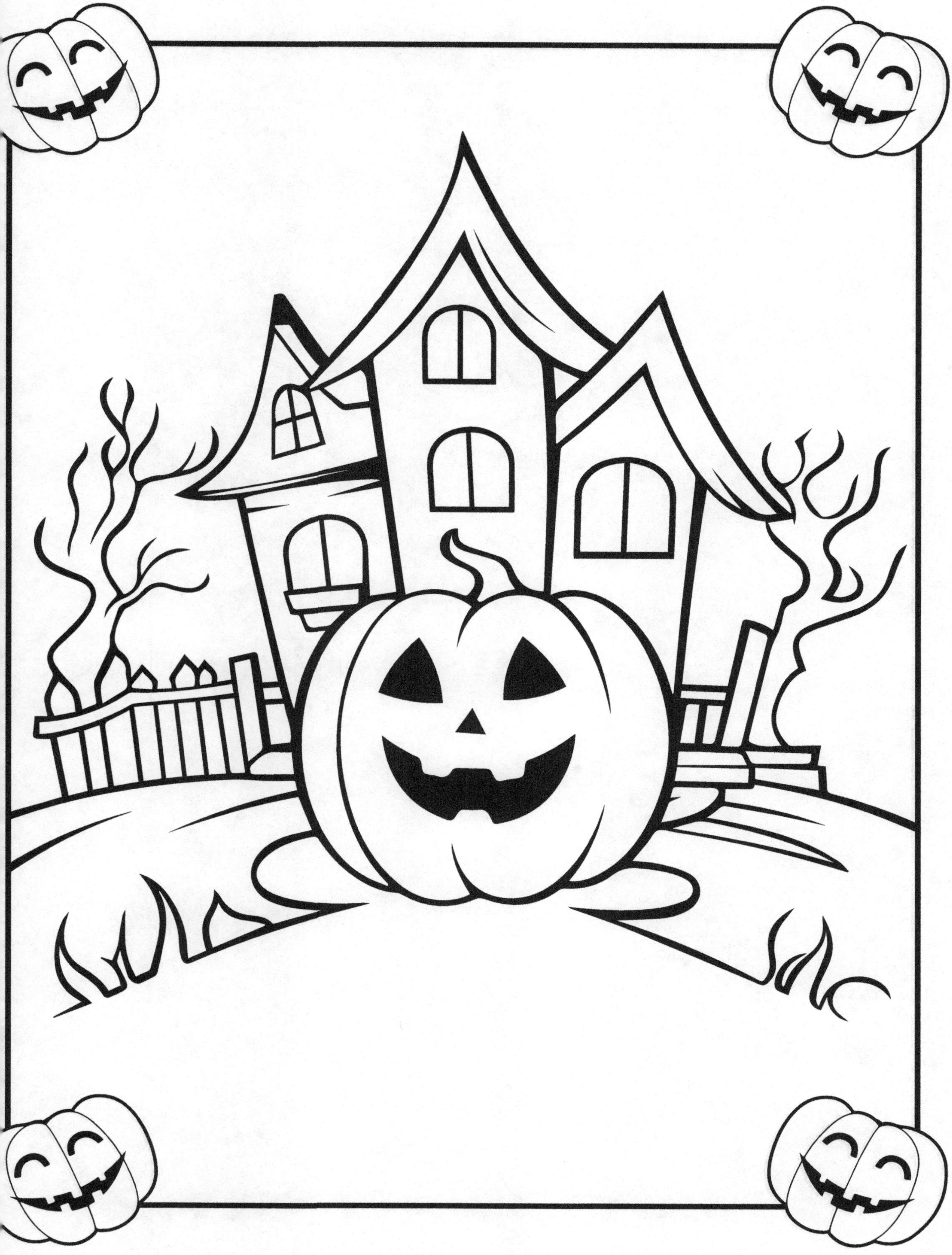

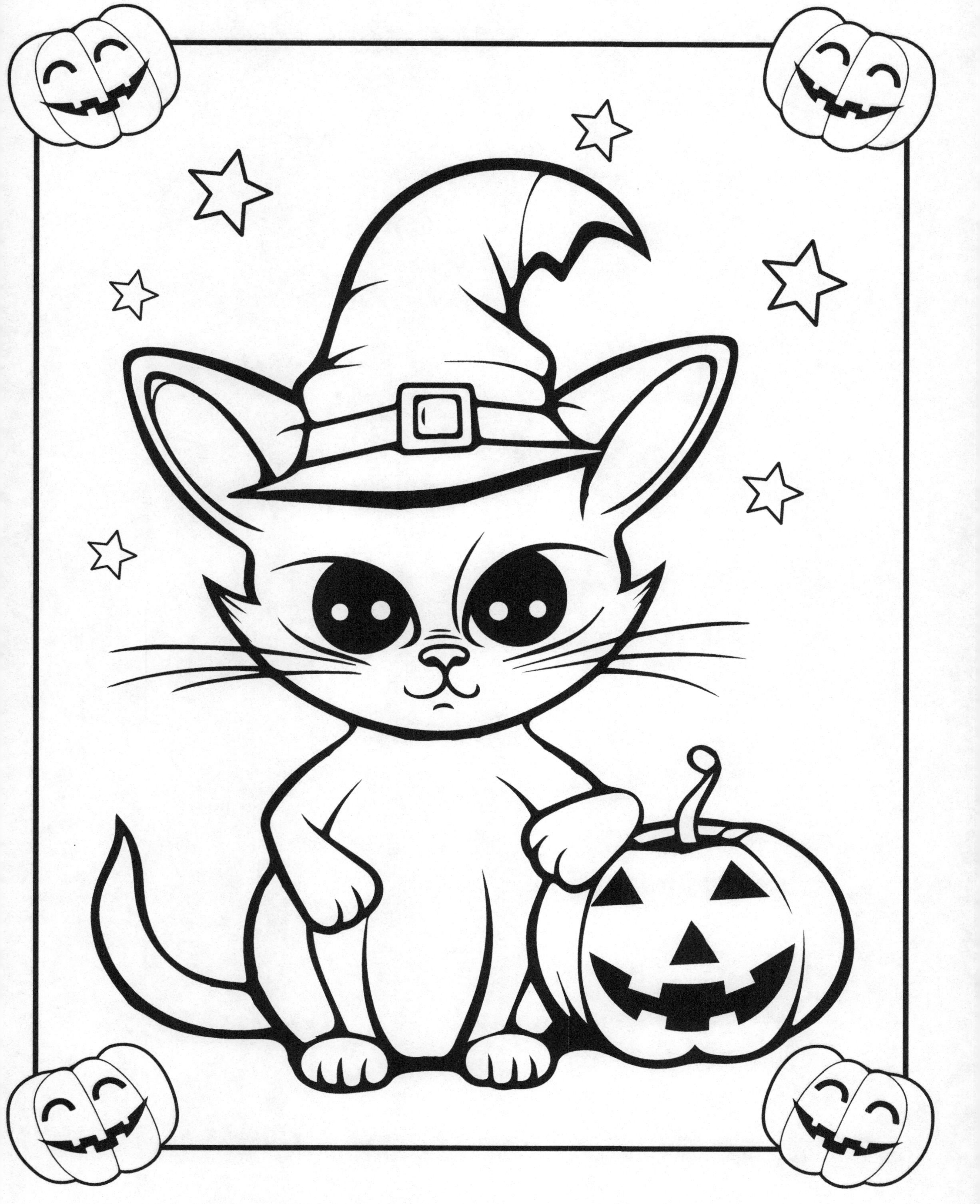

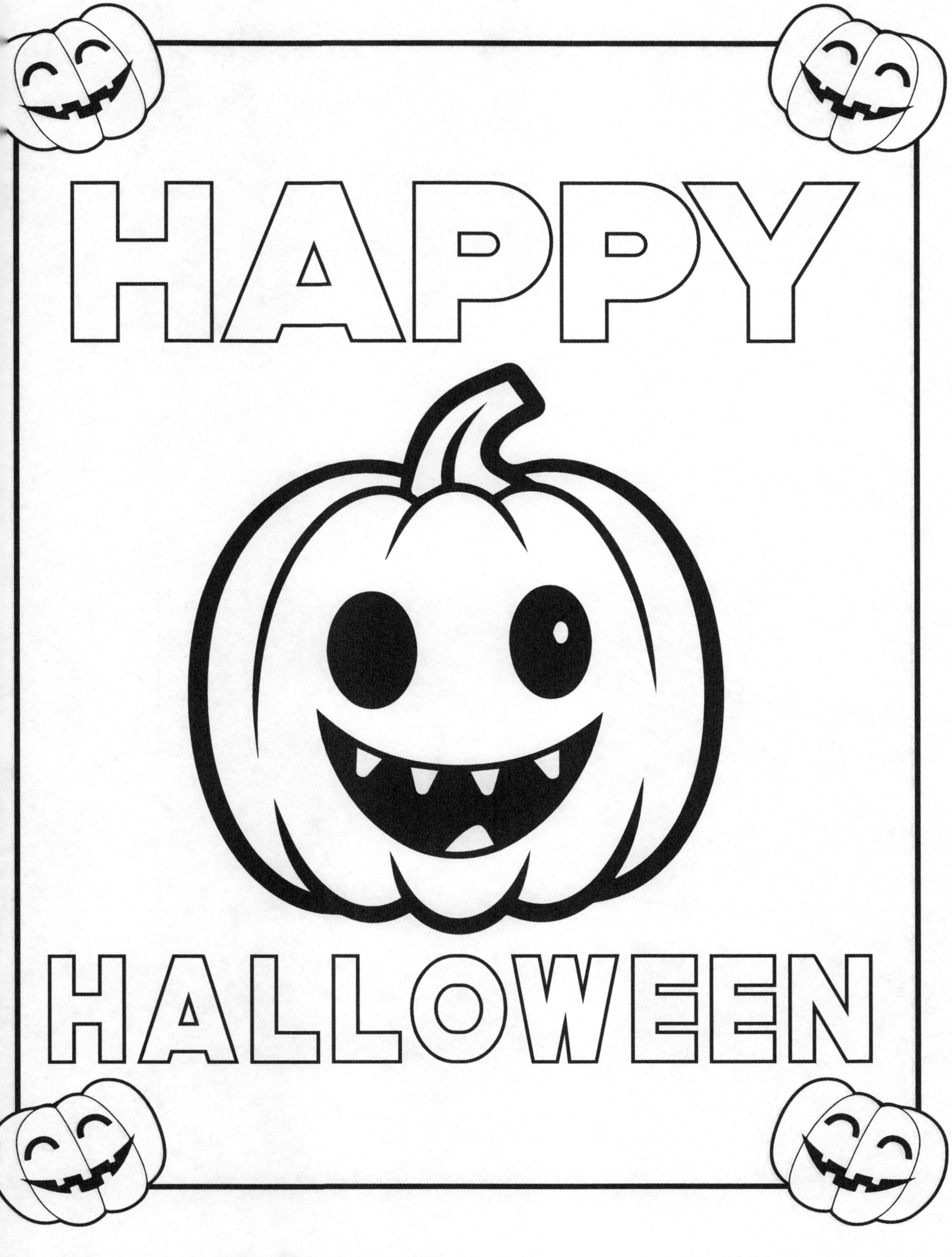
HAPPY
HALLOWEEN

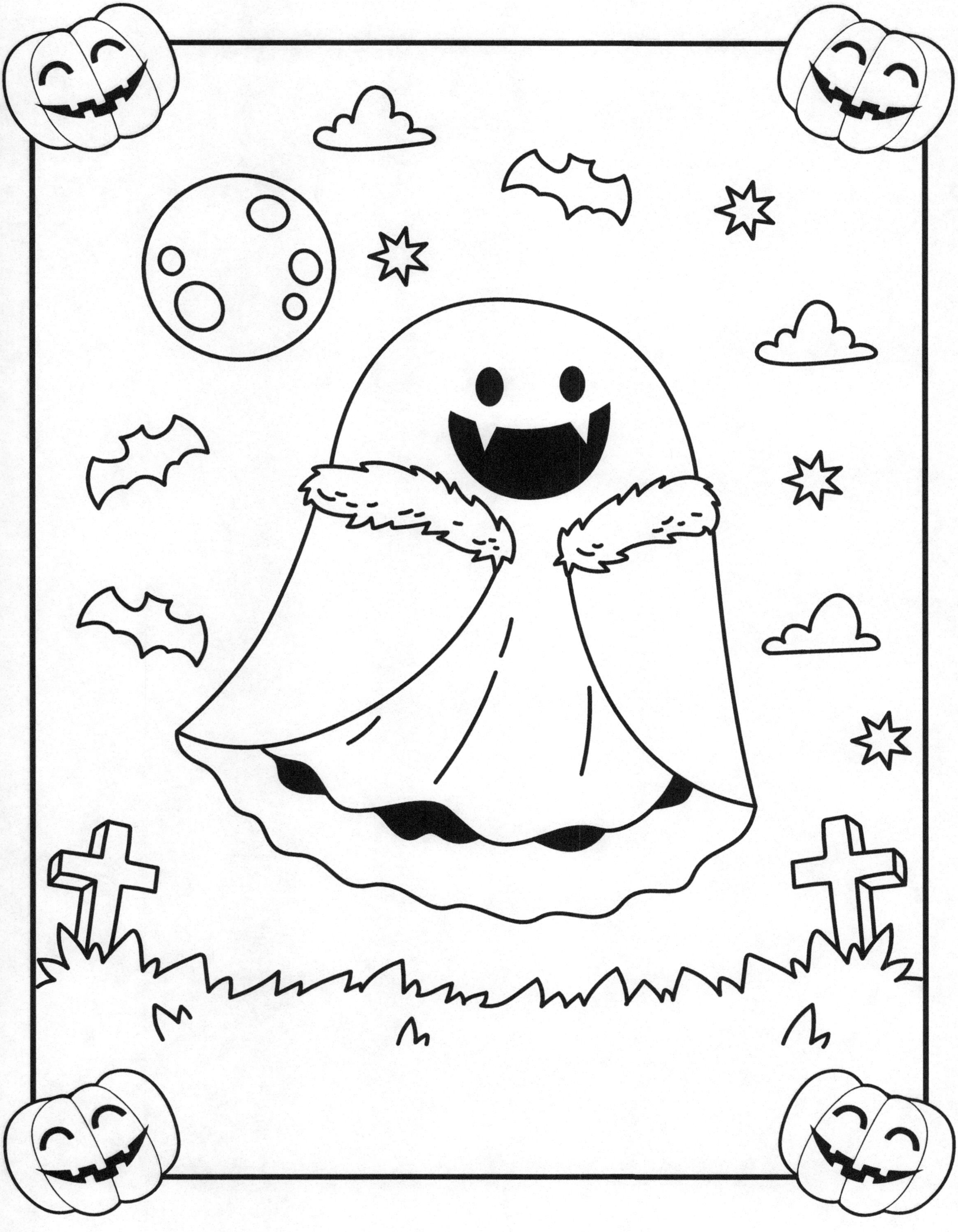

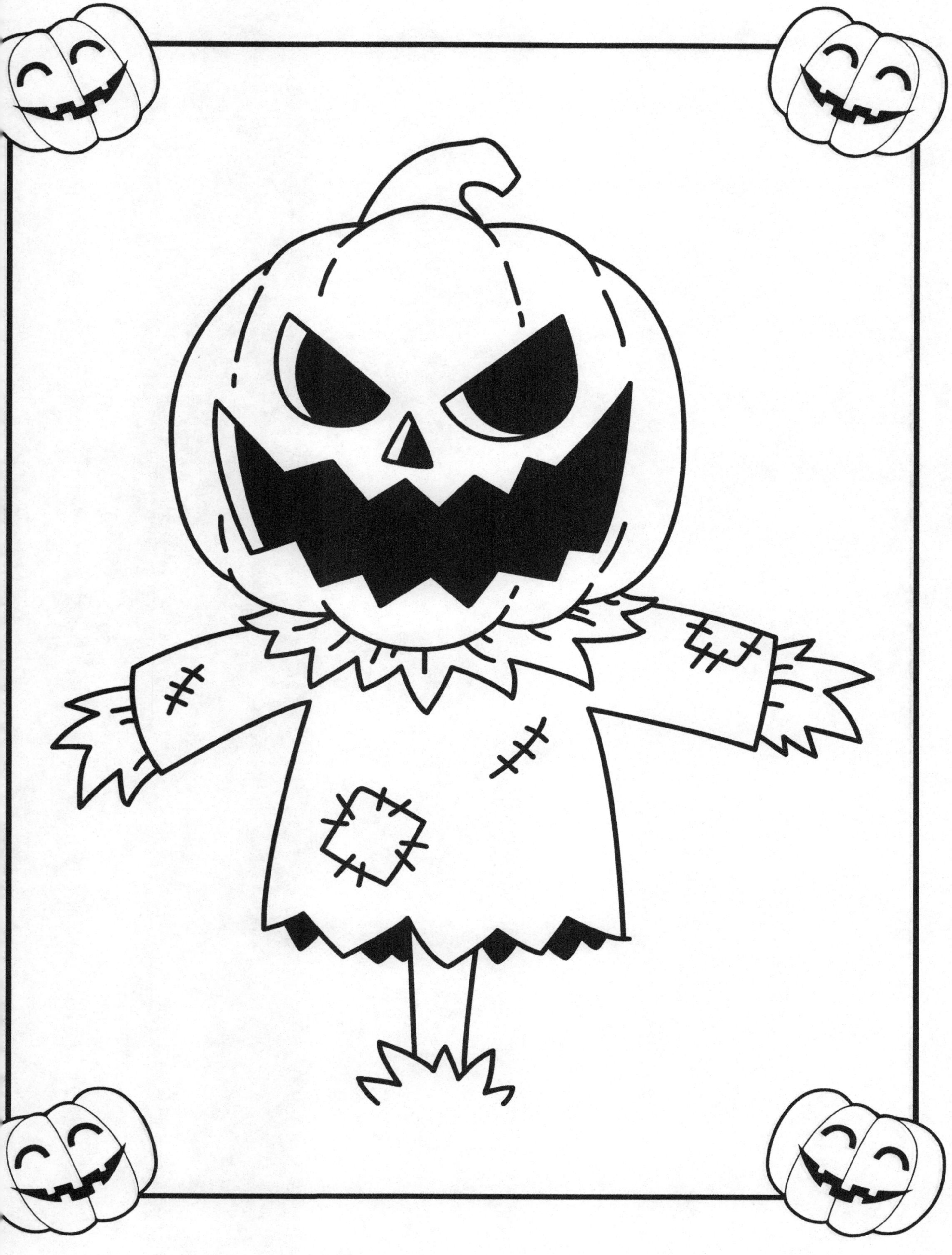

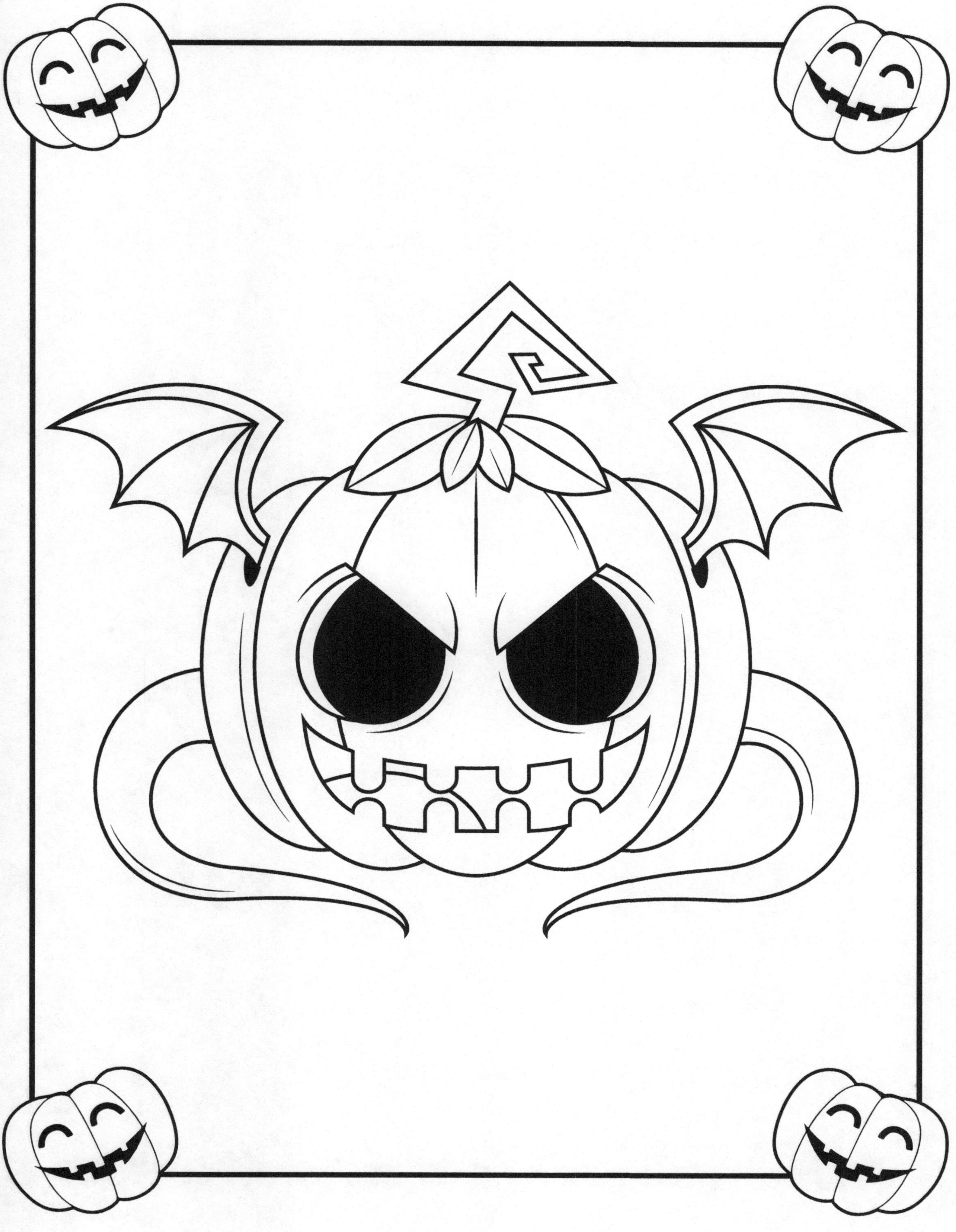

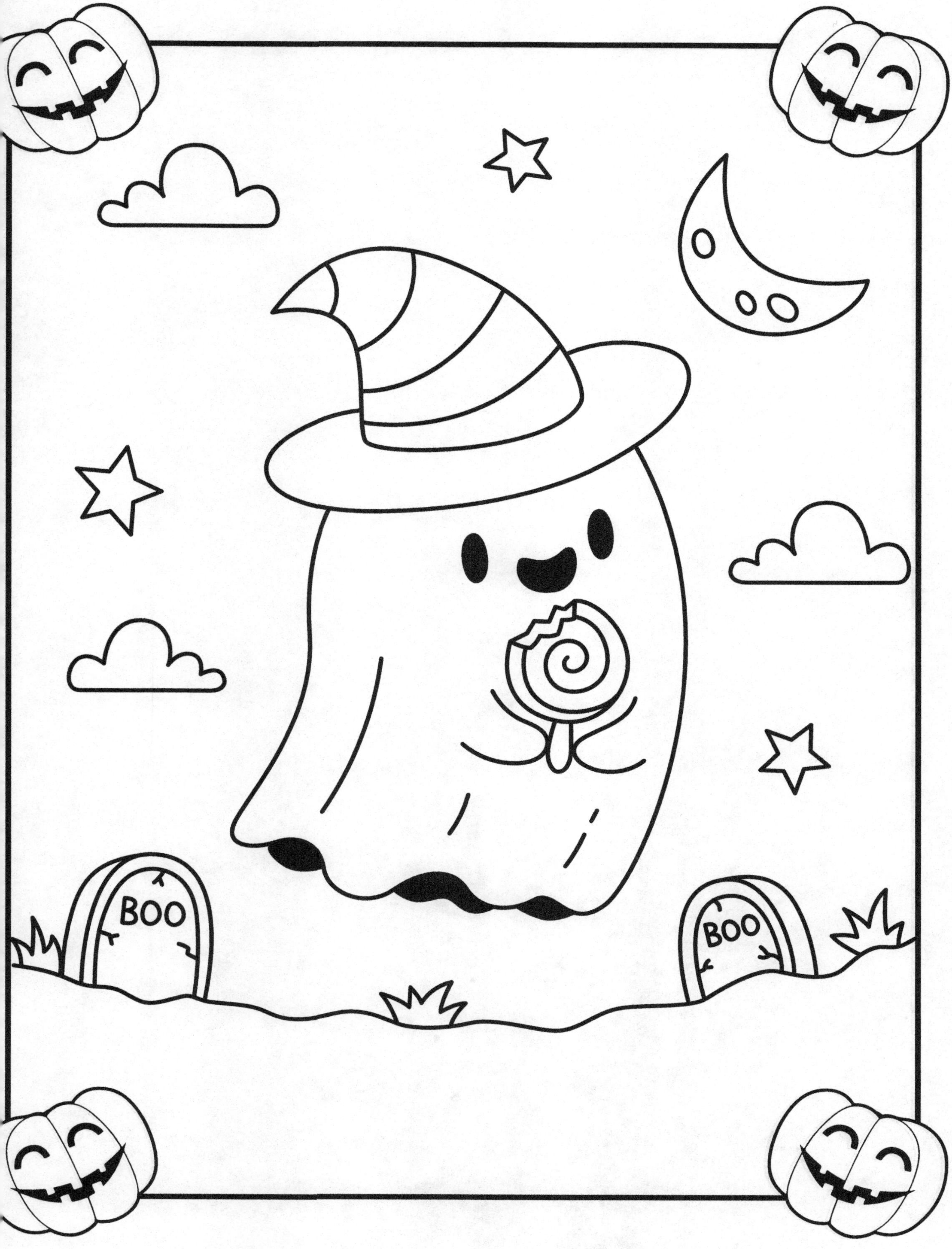
BOO
BOO

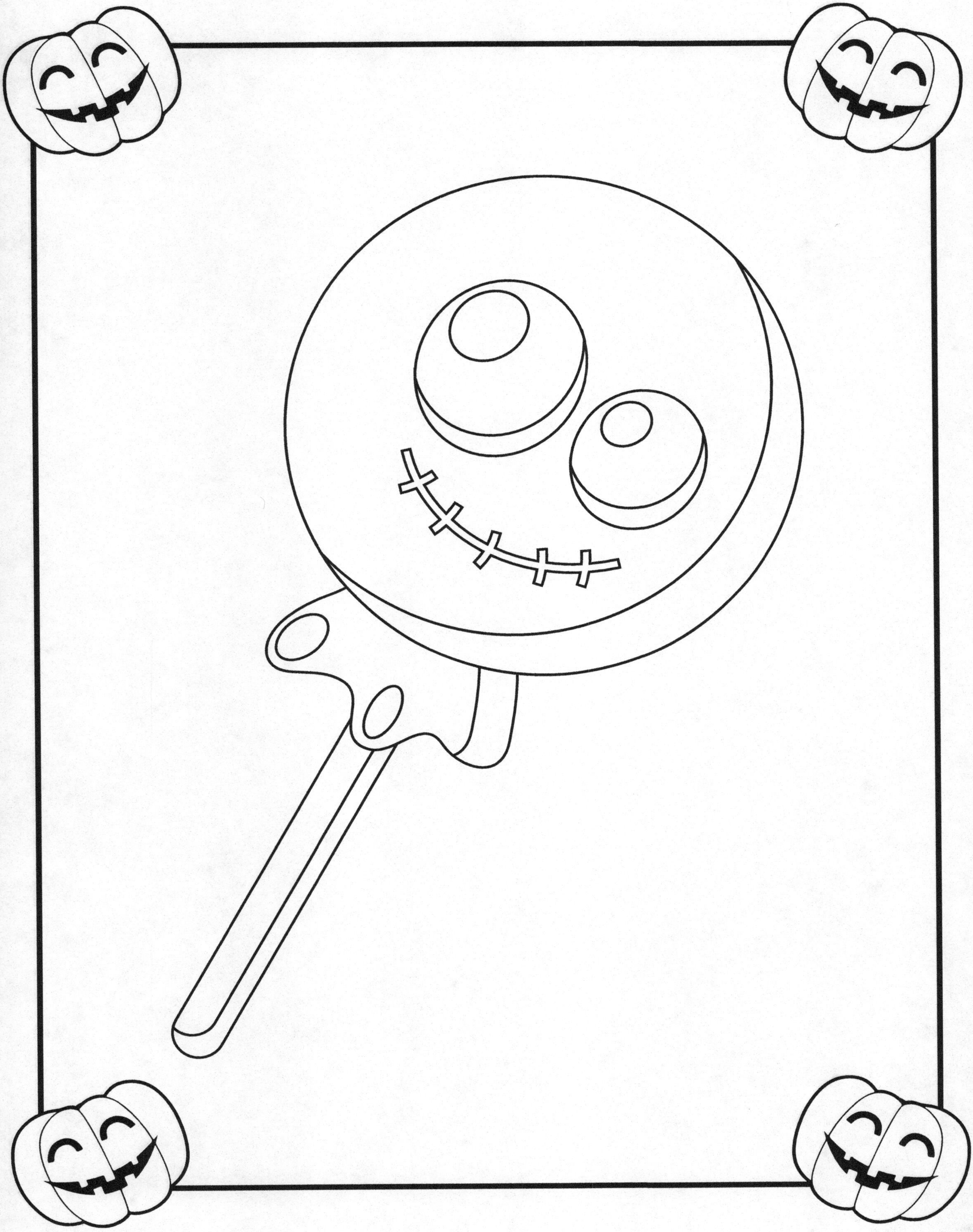

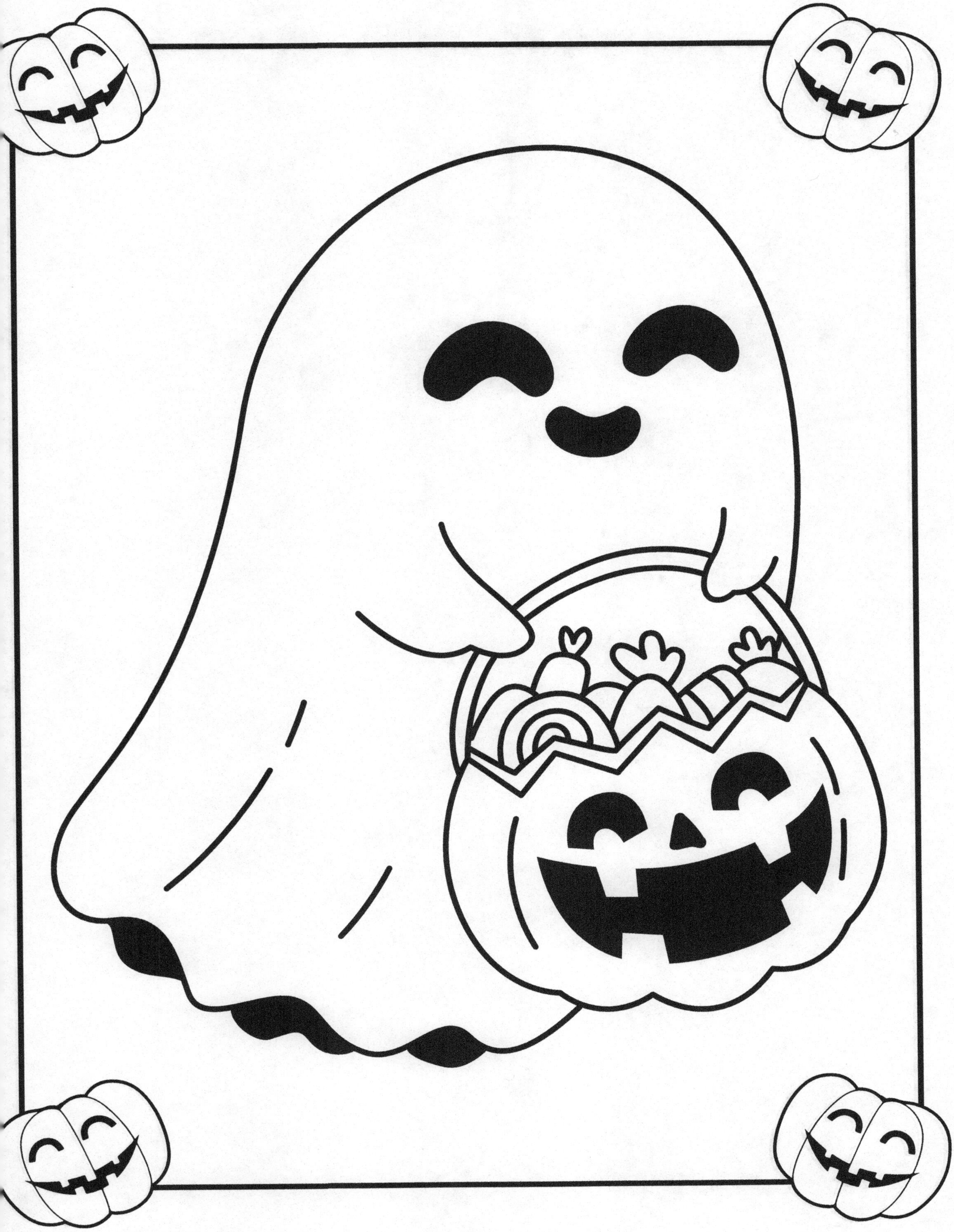

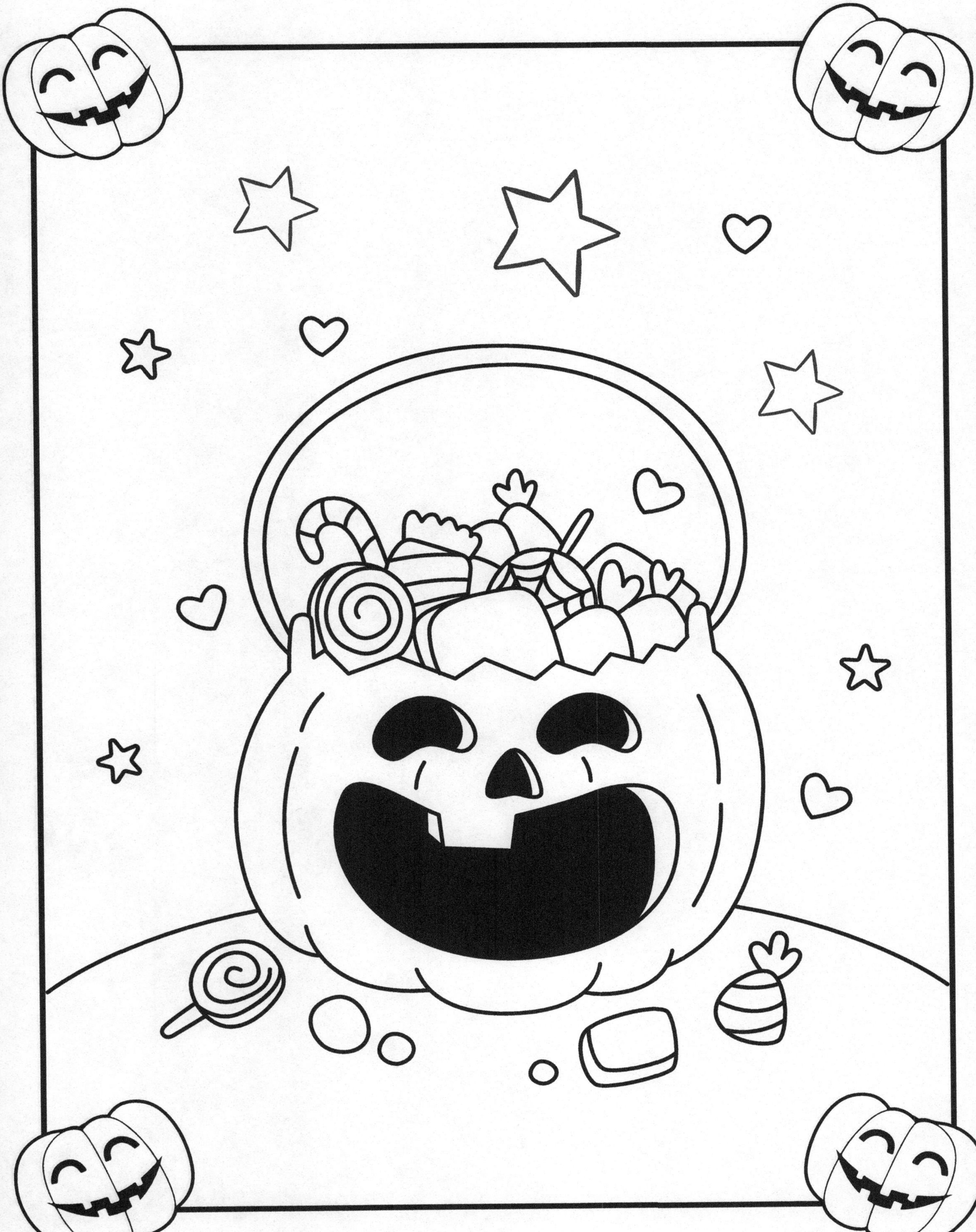

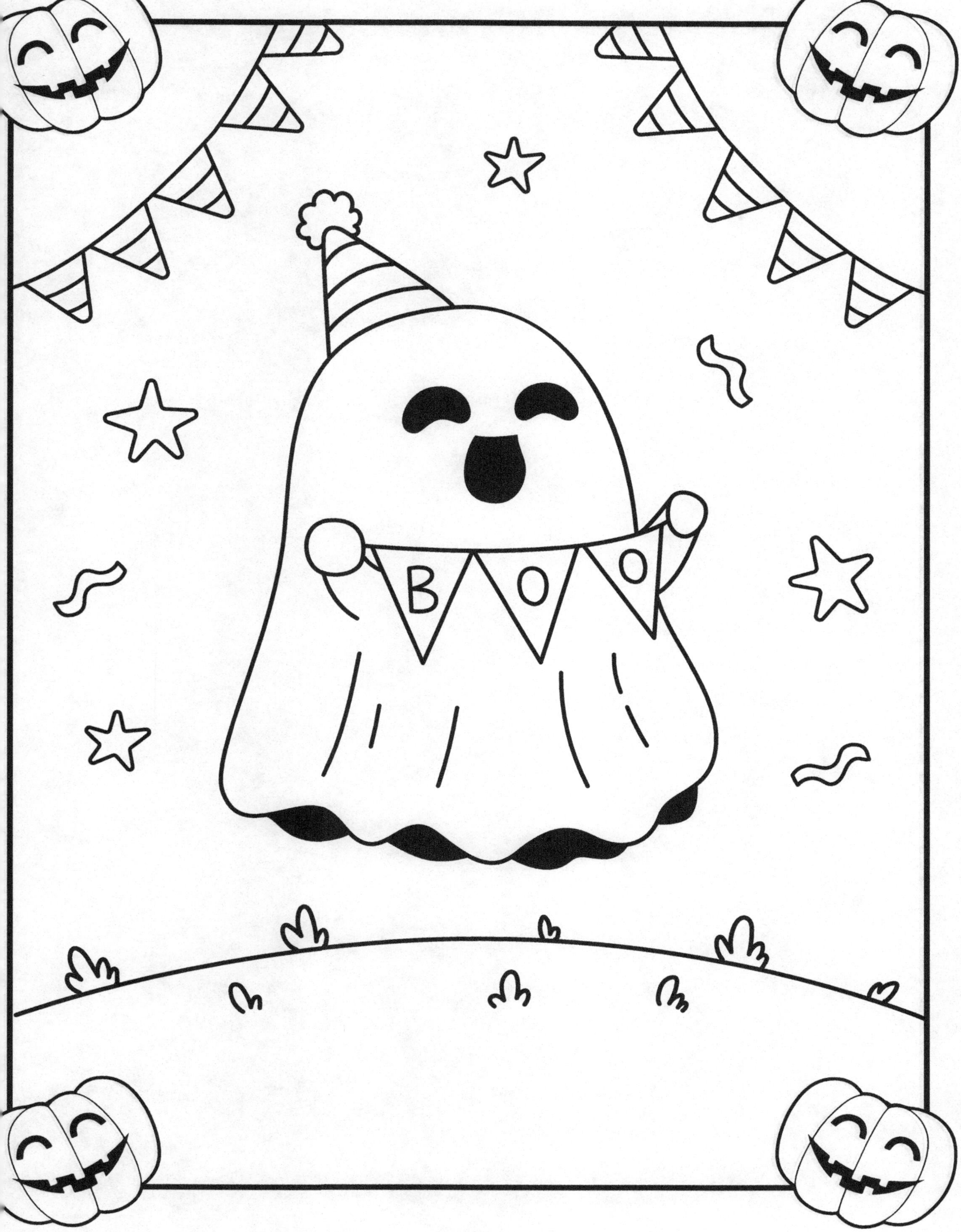
BOO

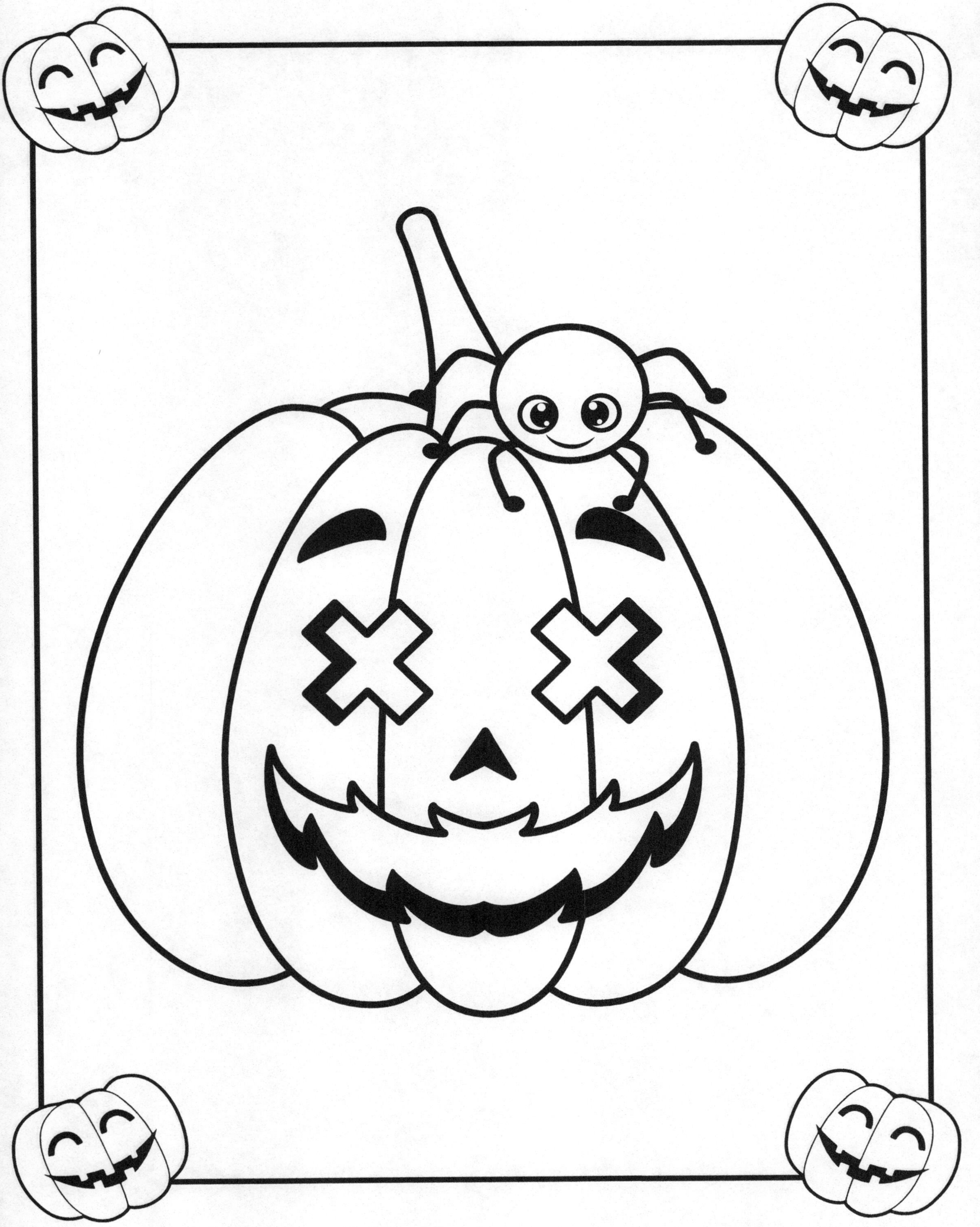

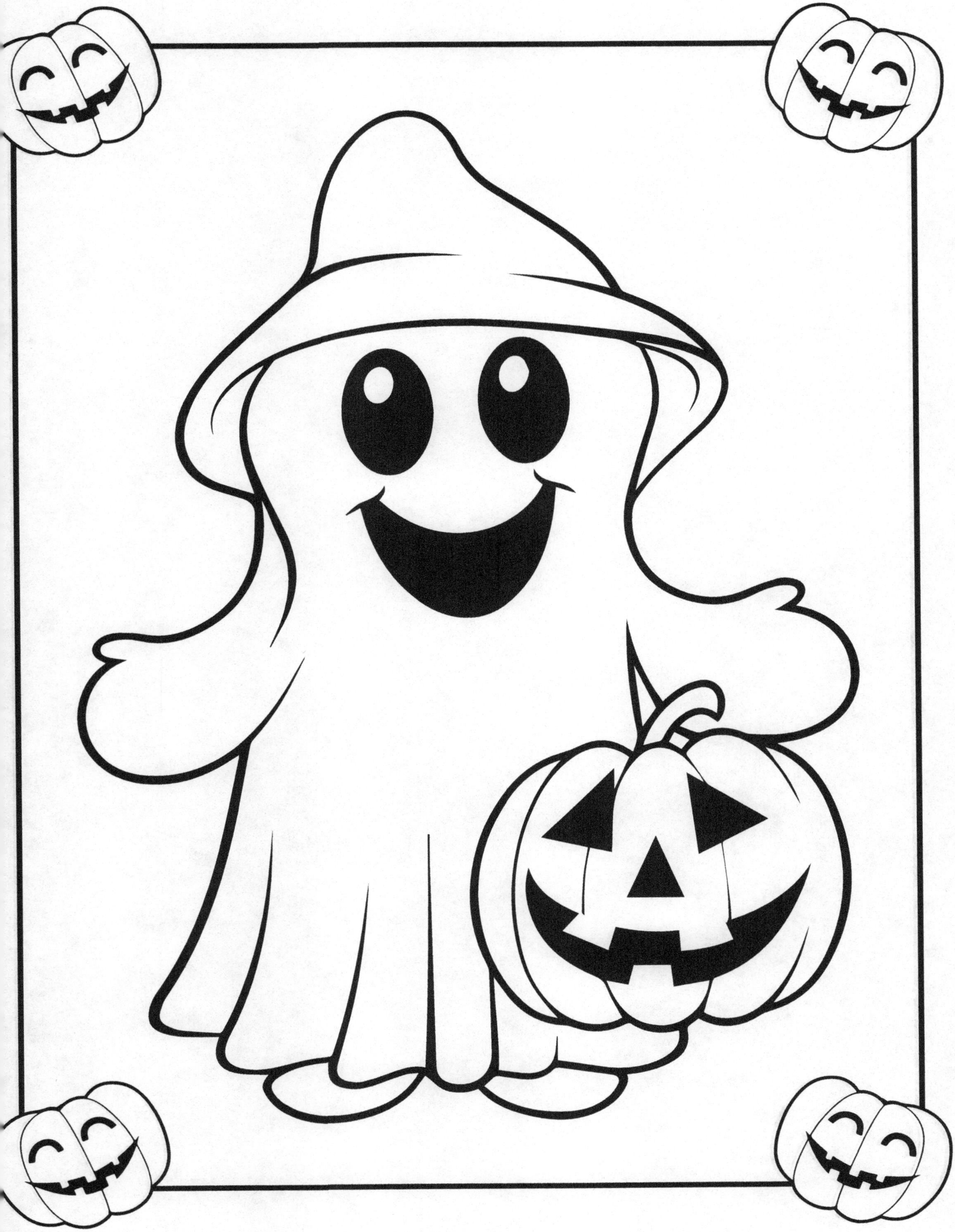

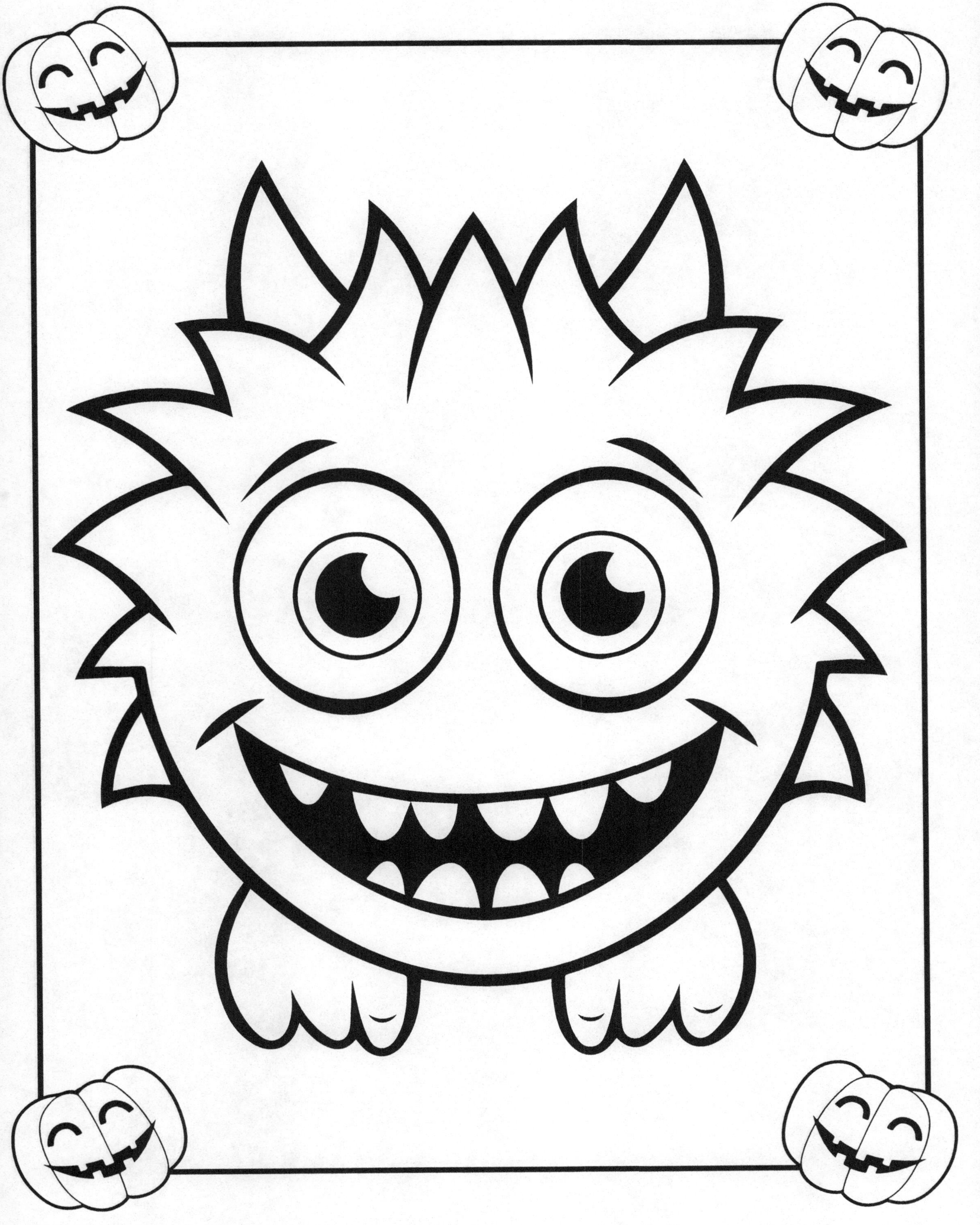

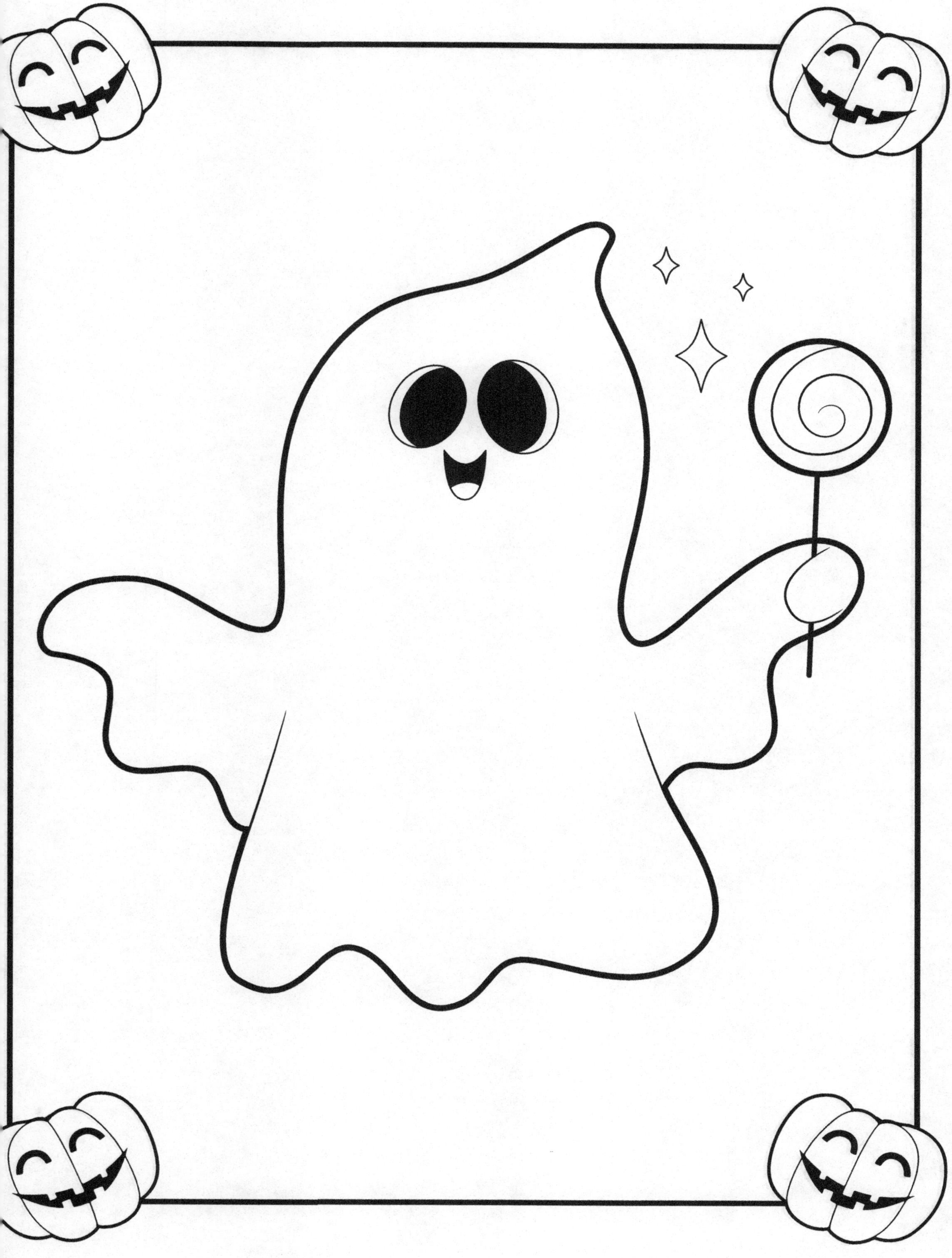

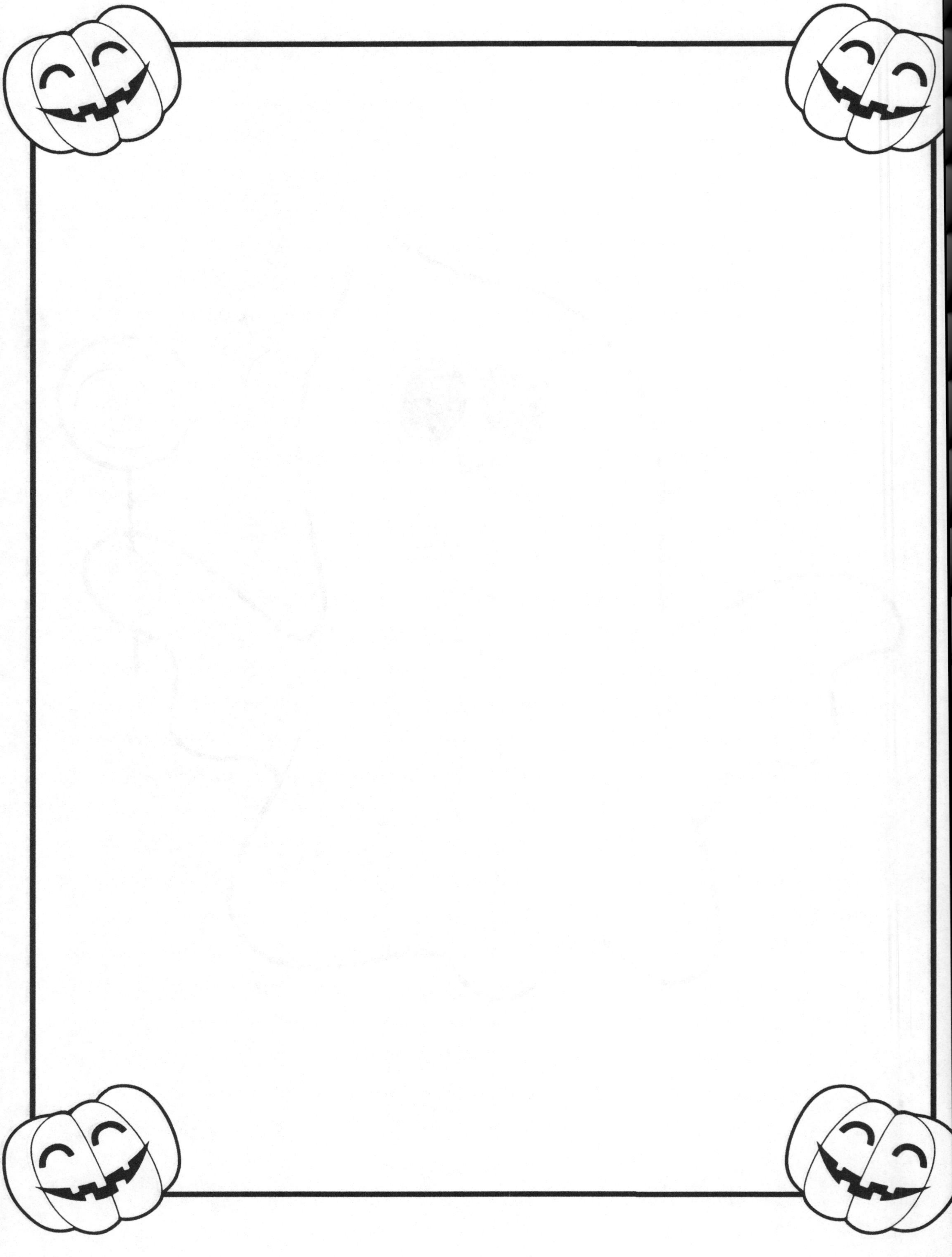

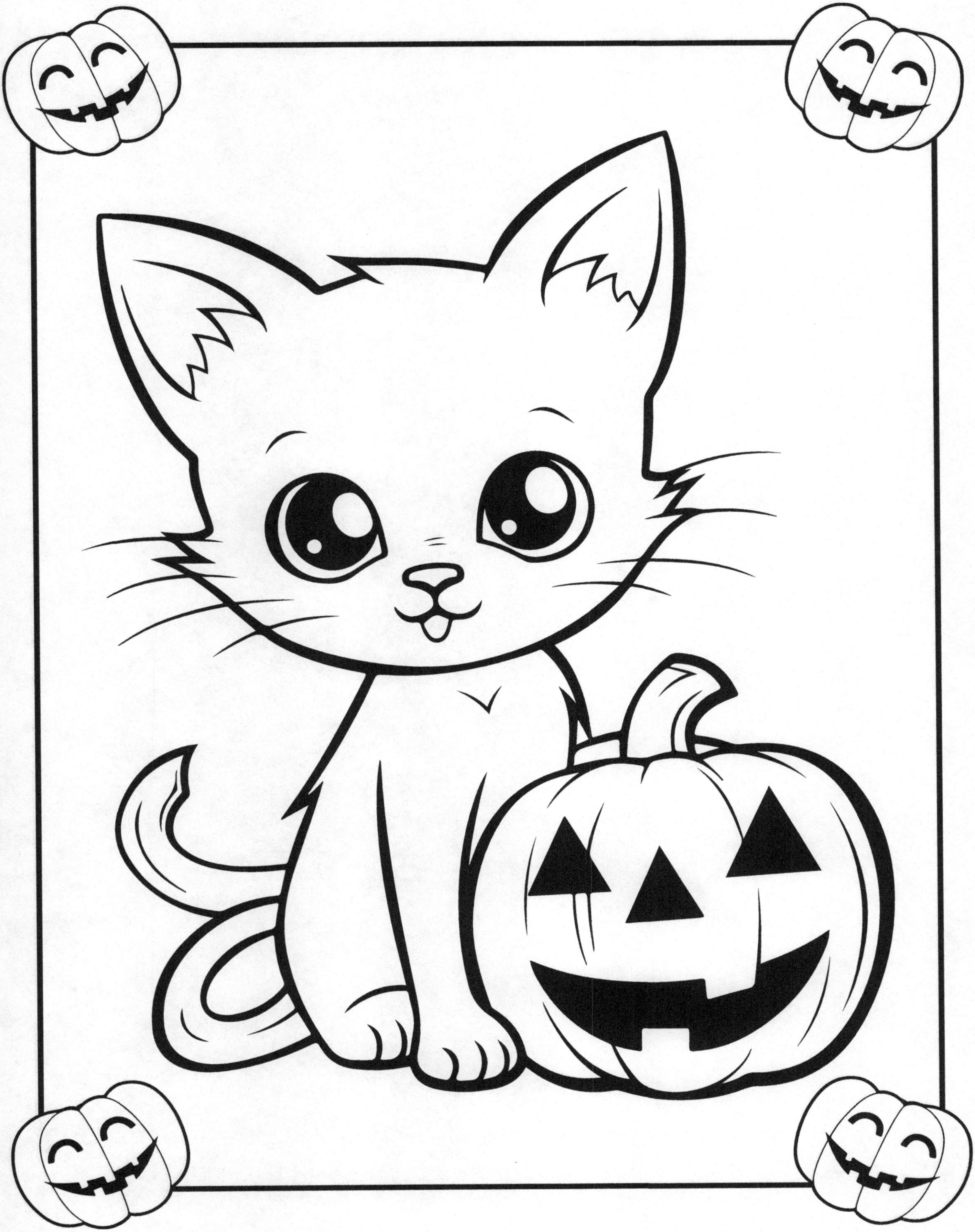

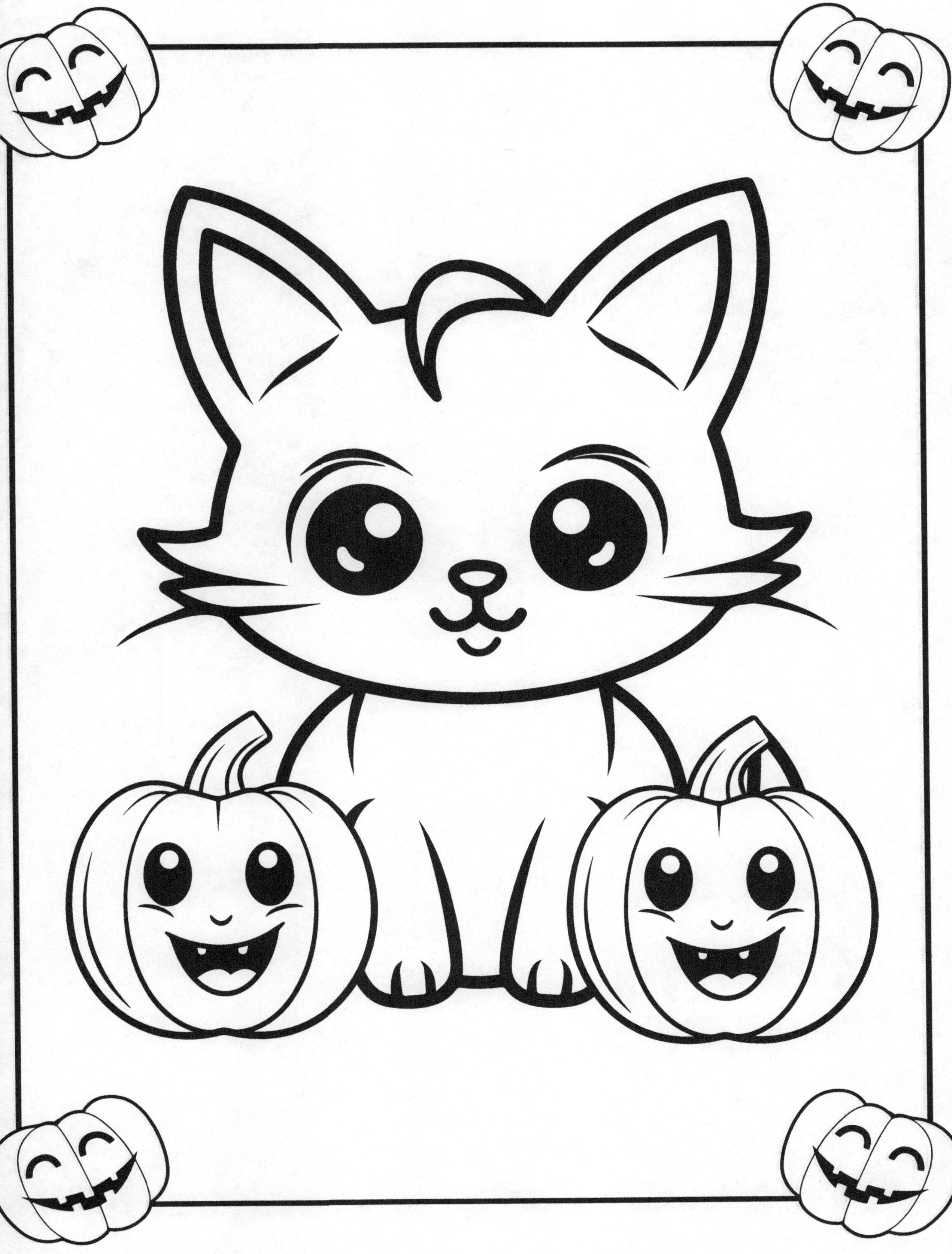

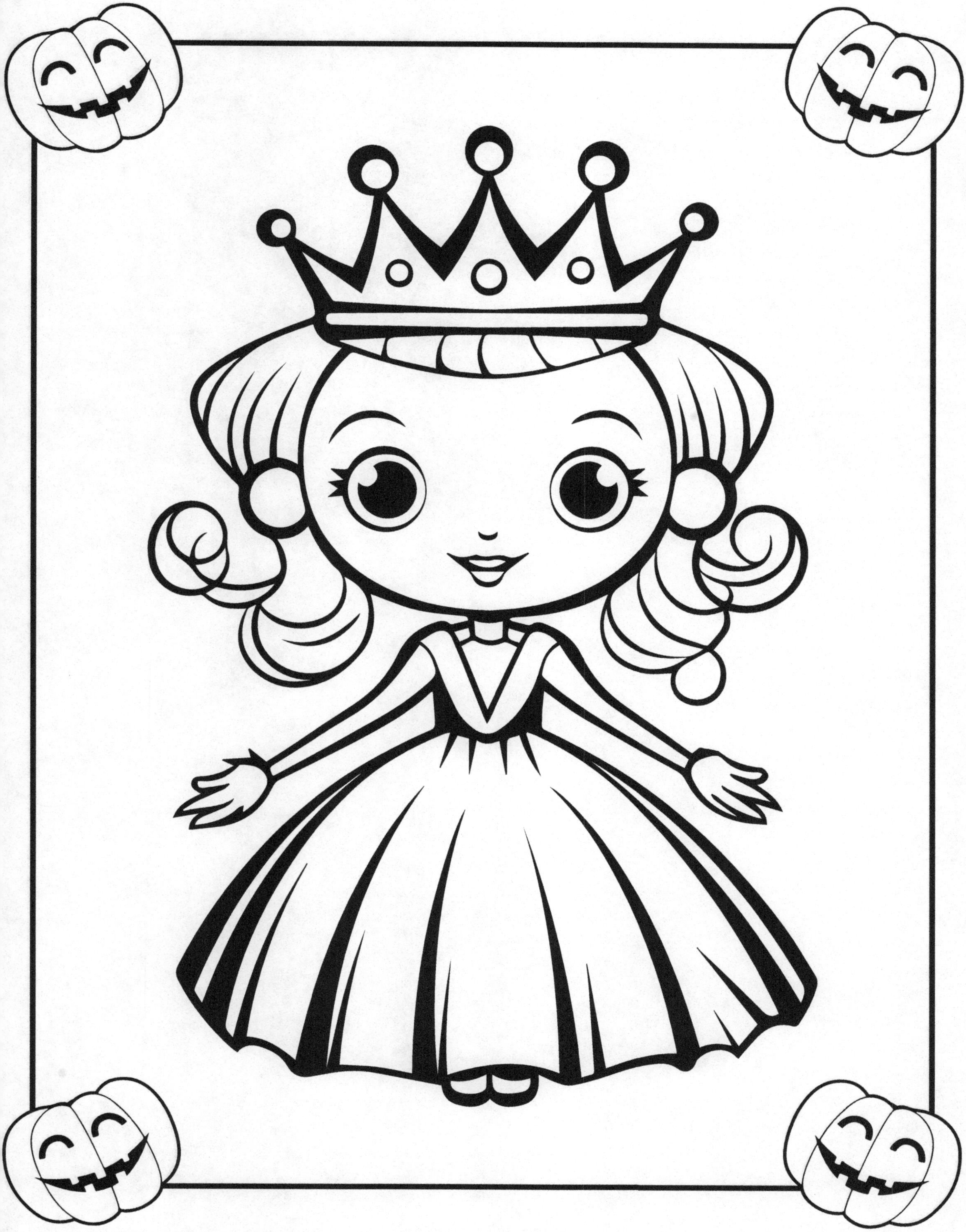

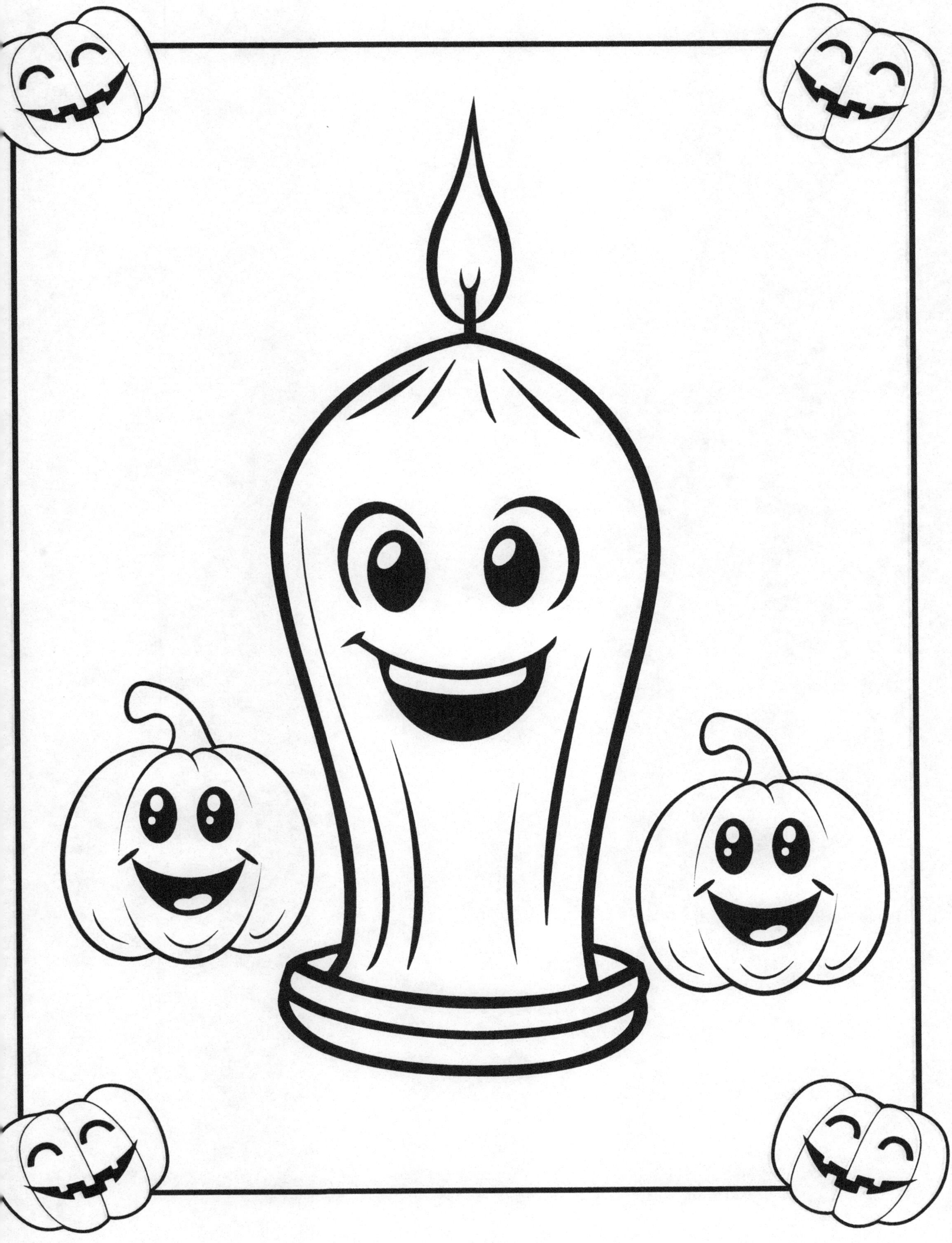

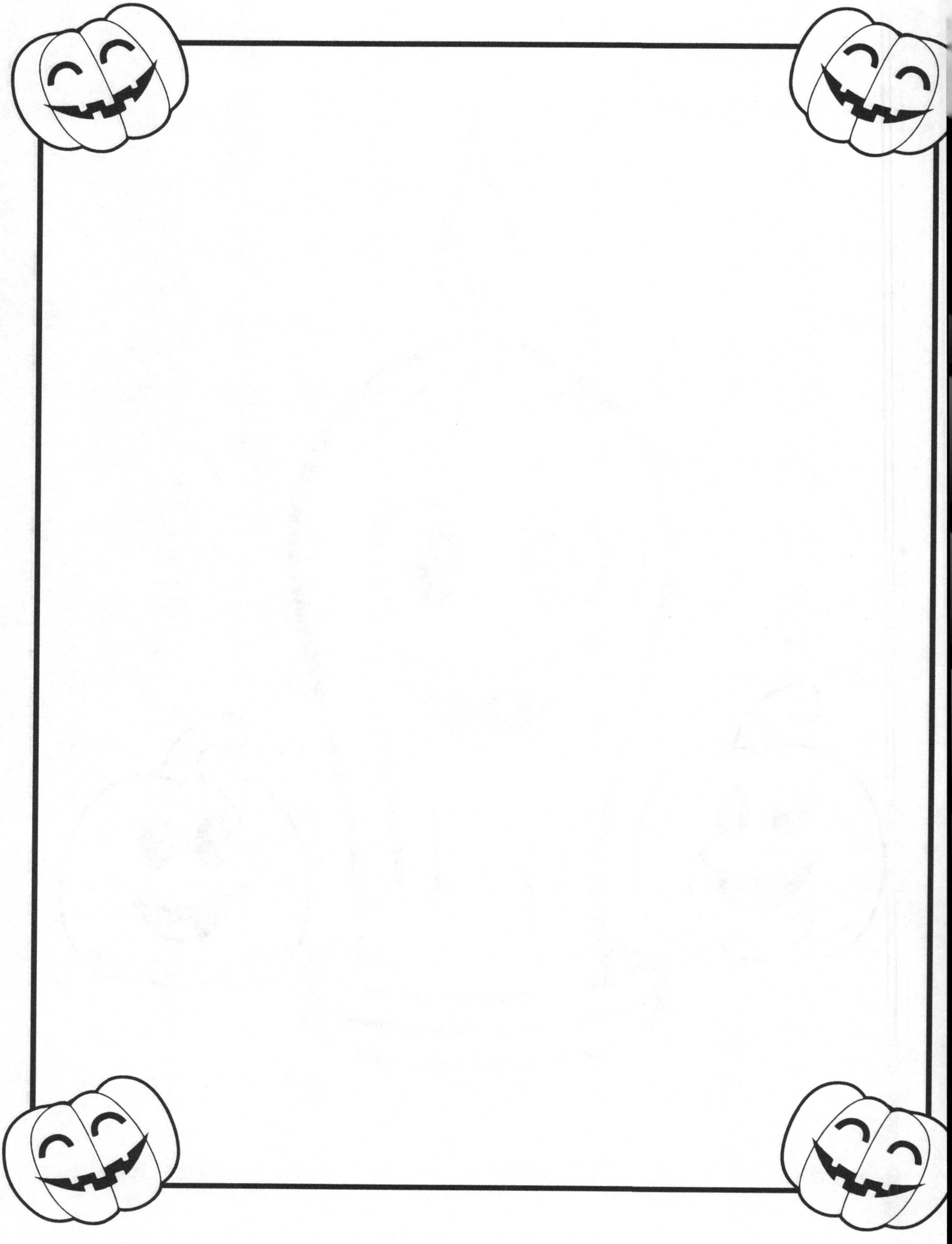

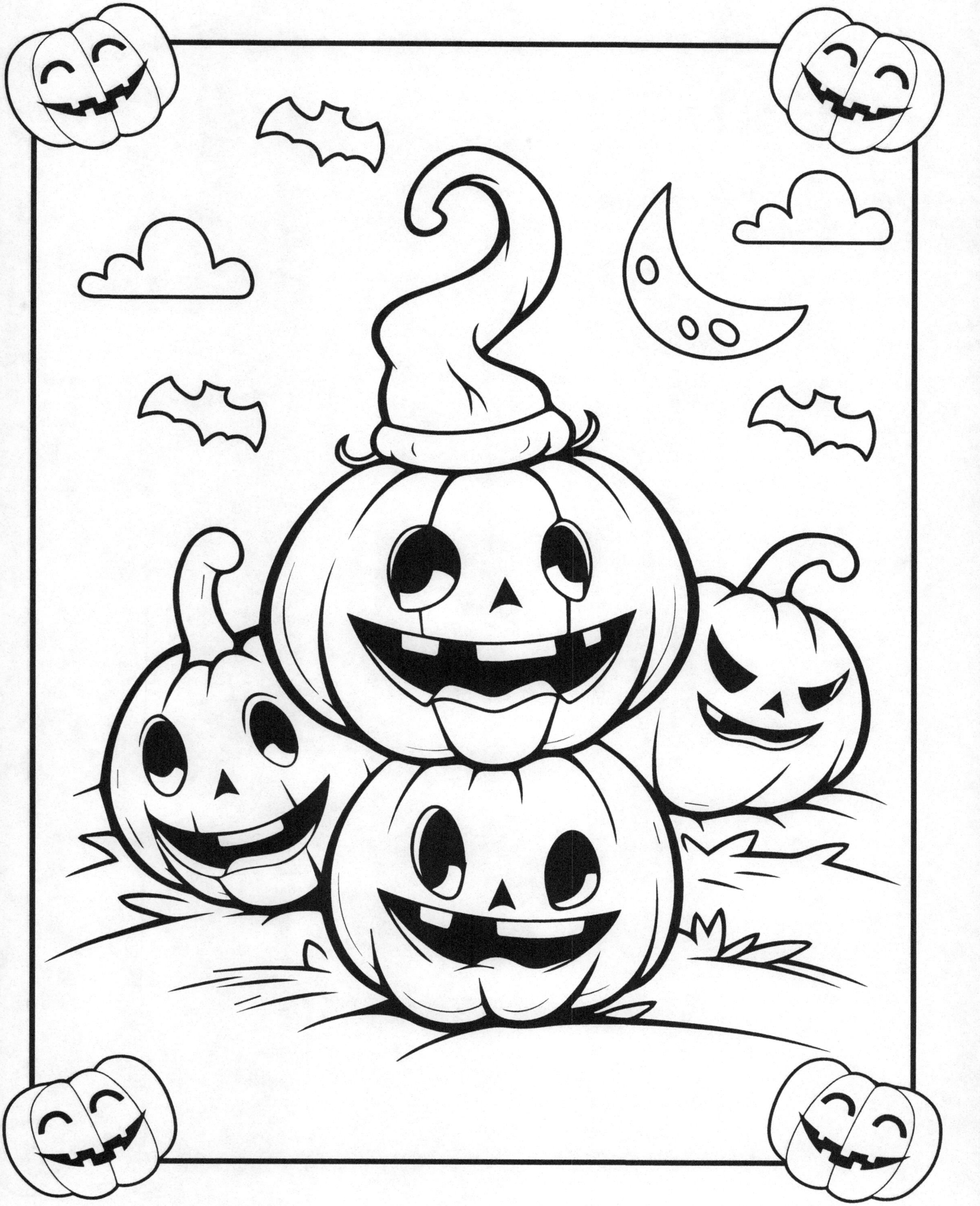

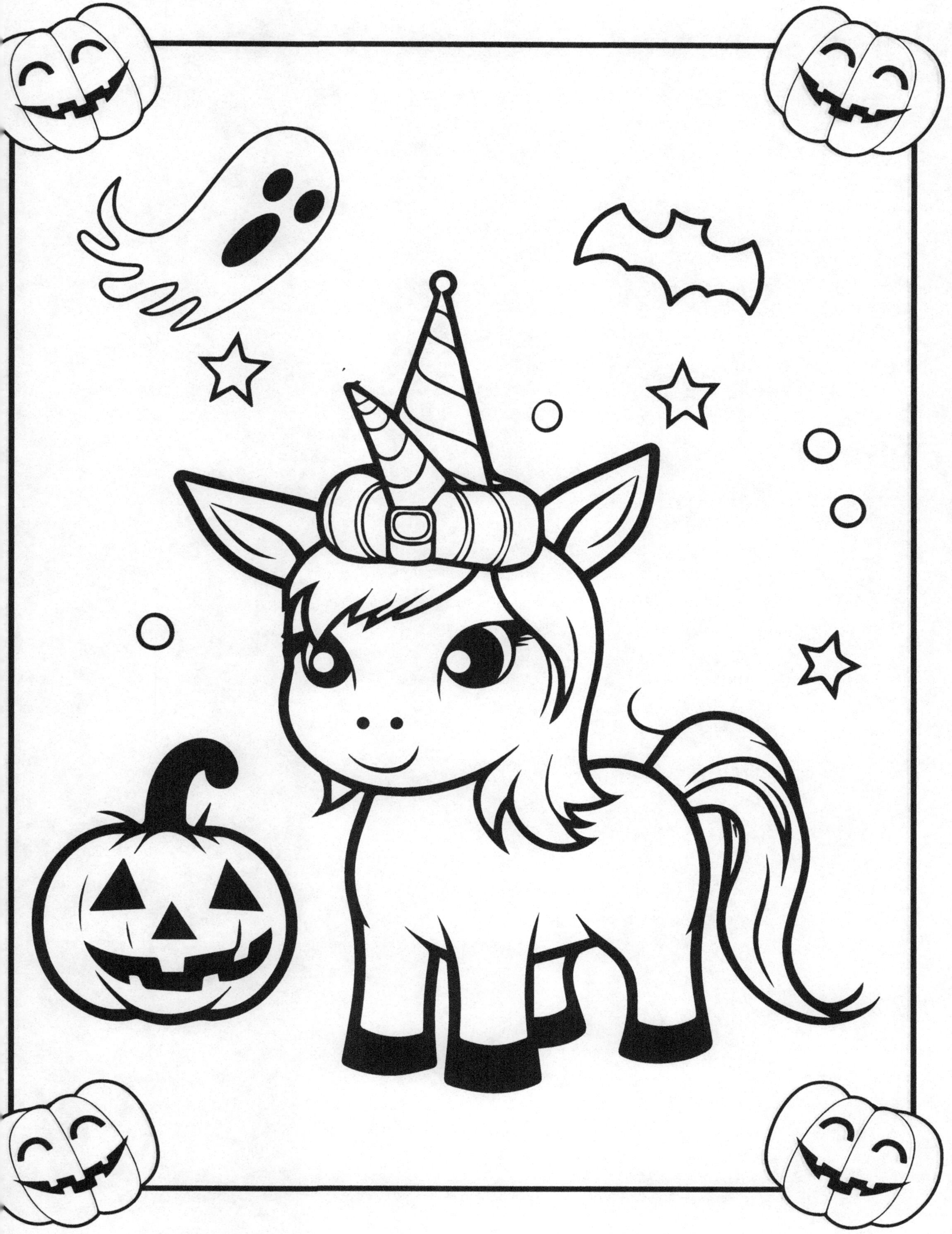

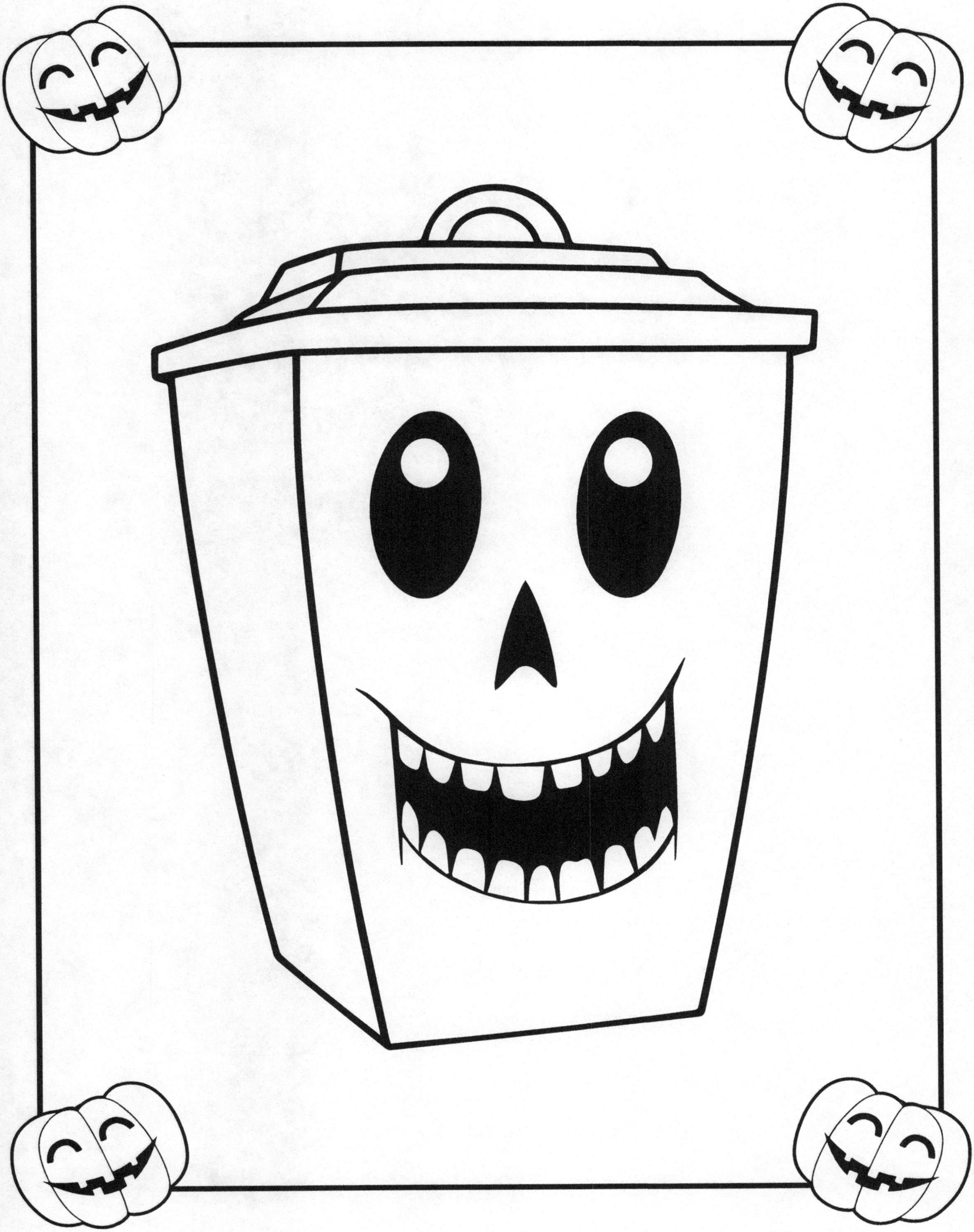

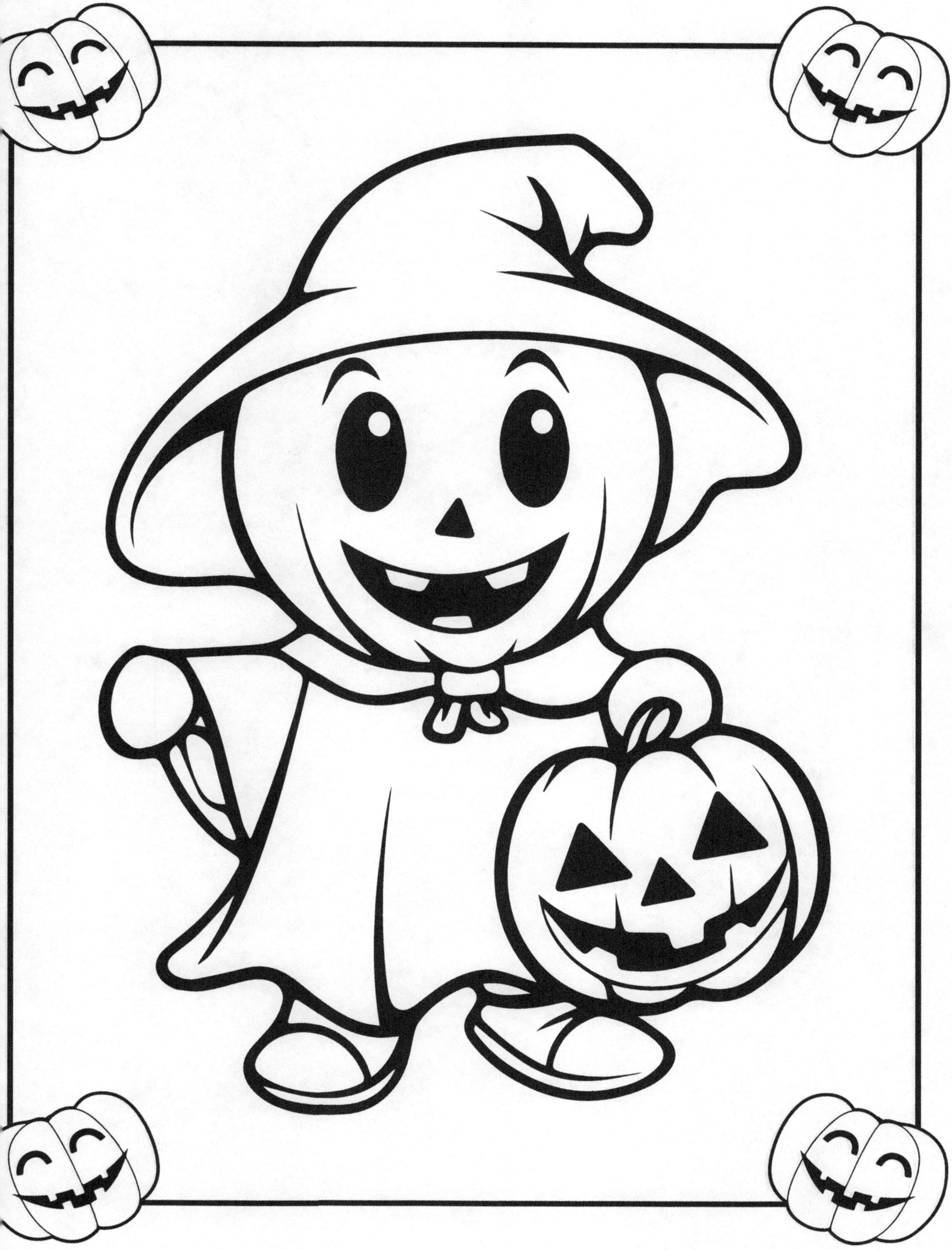

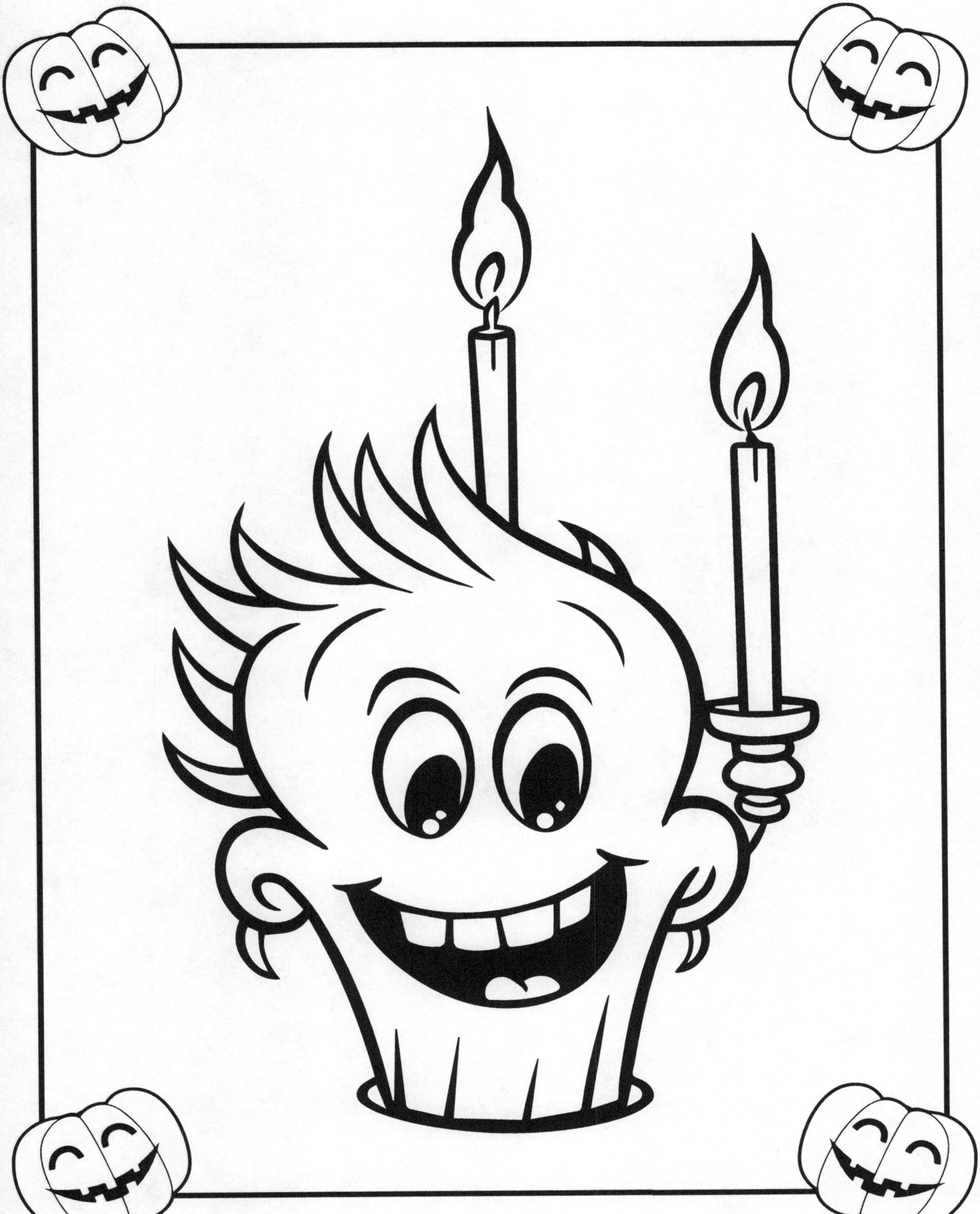

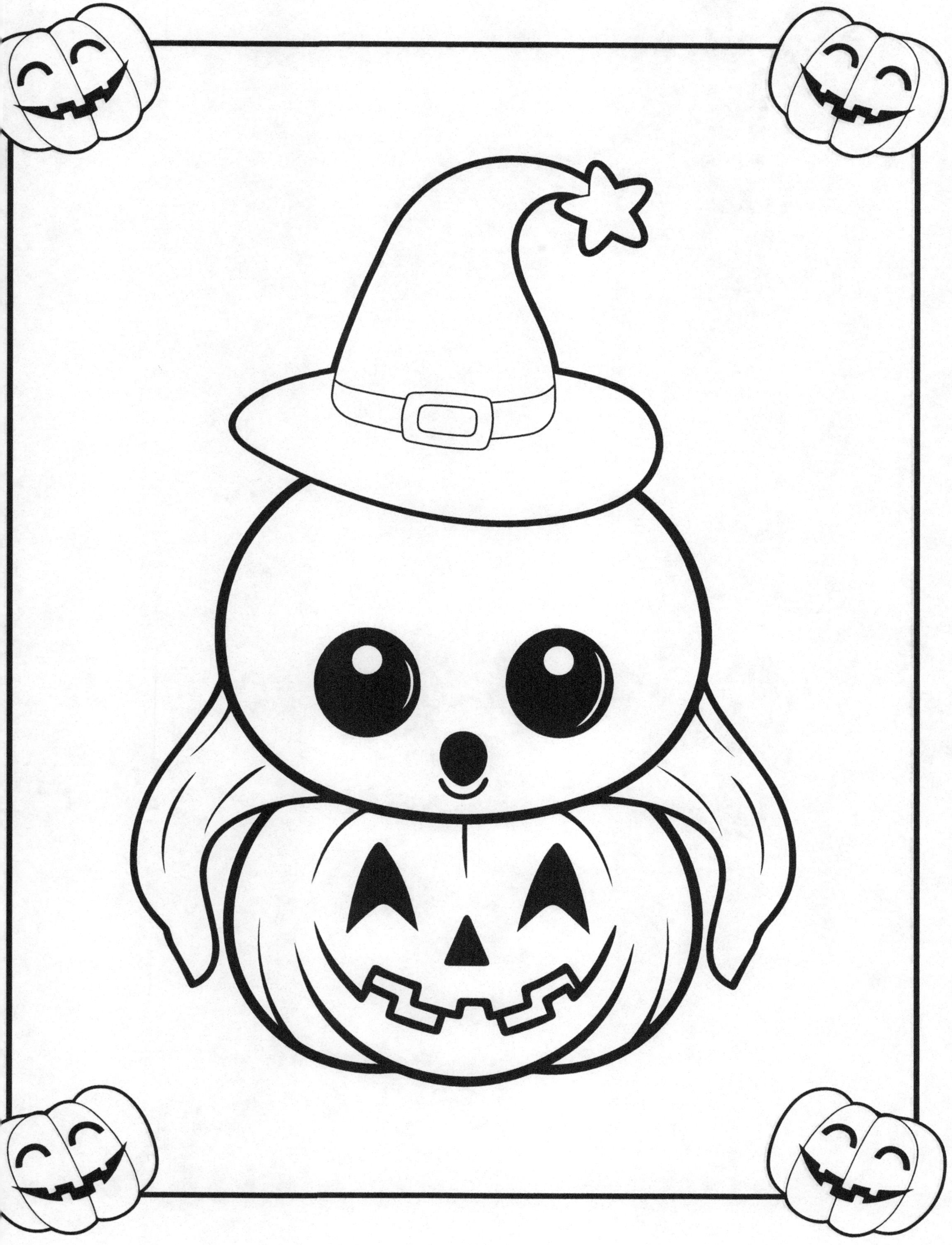

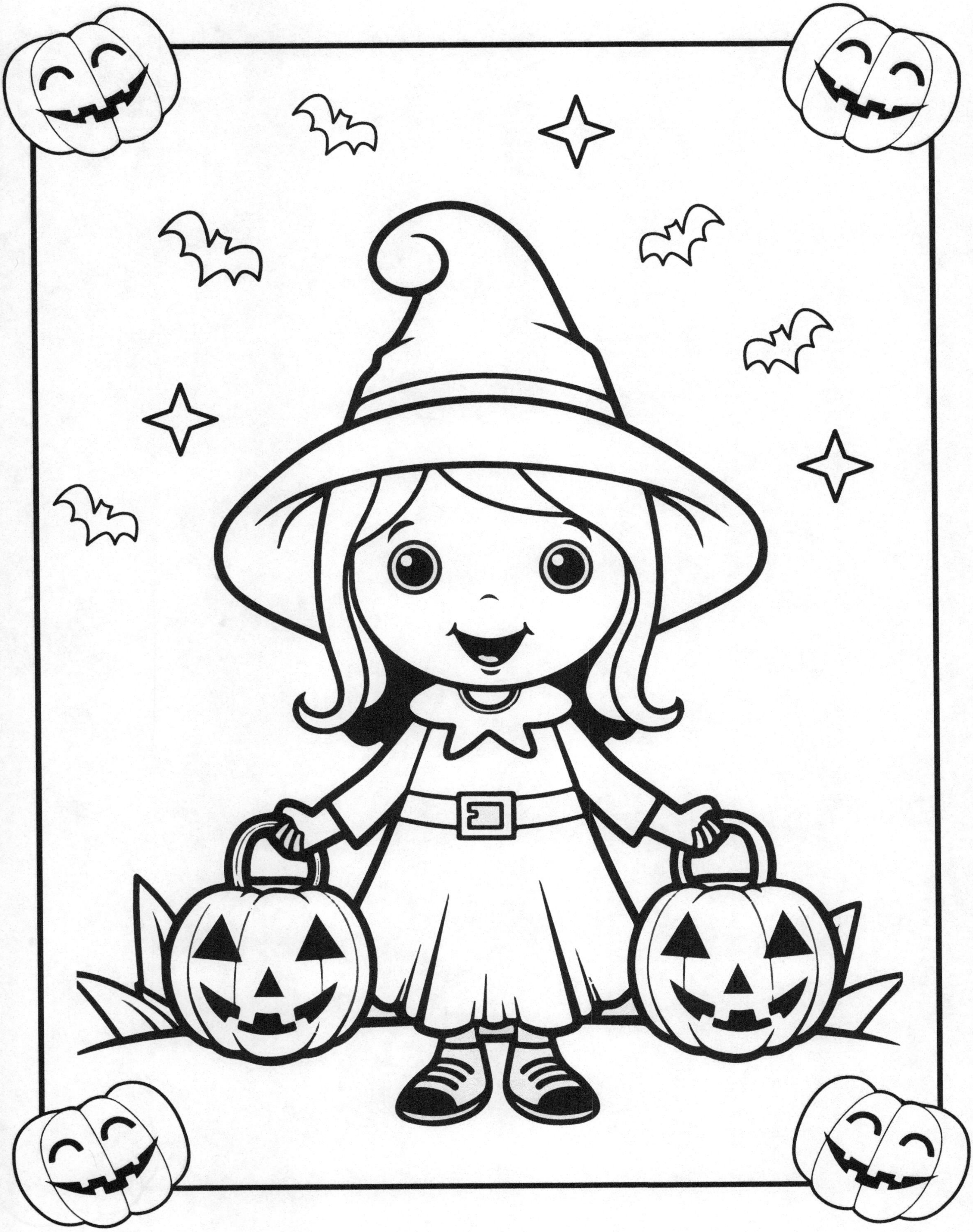

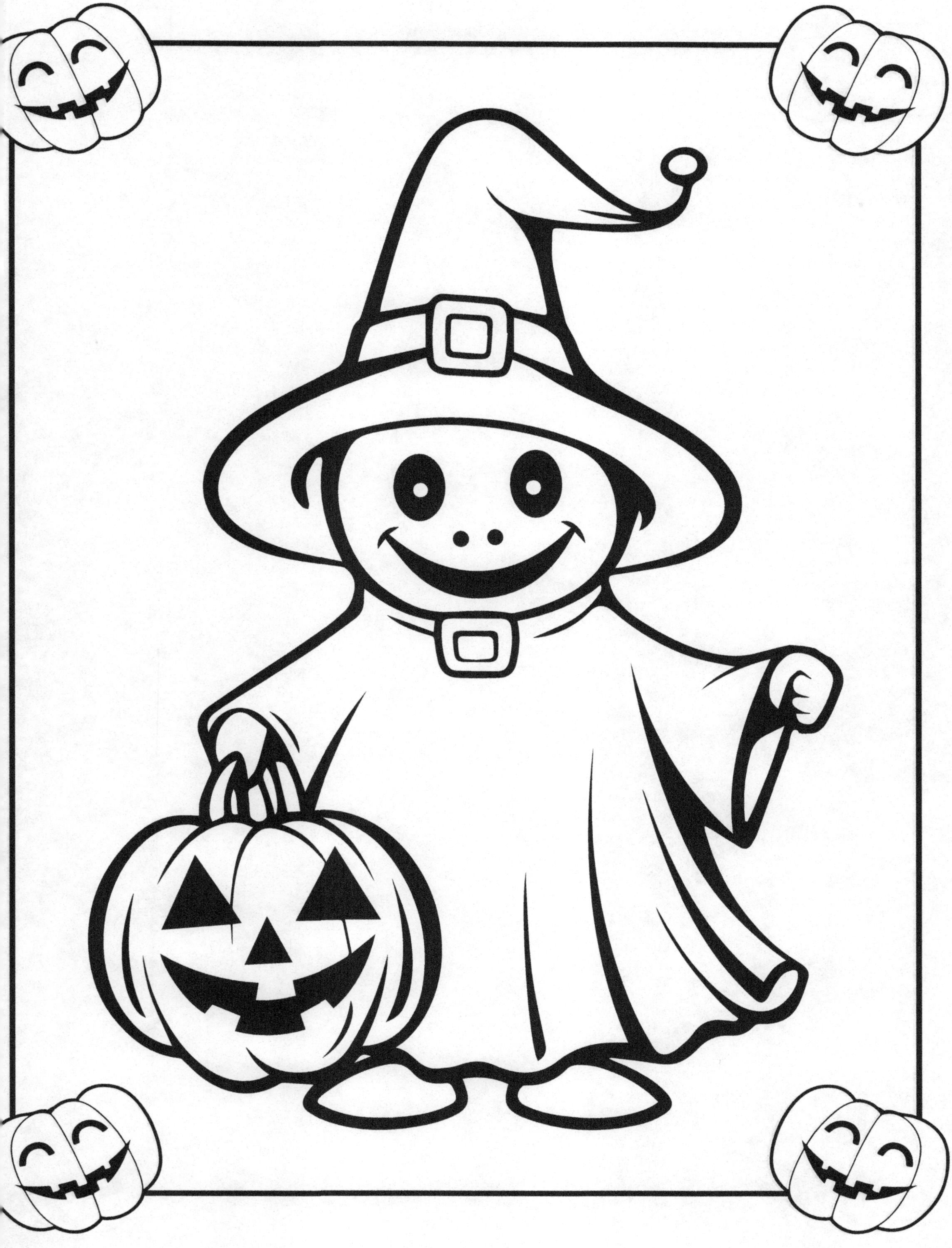

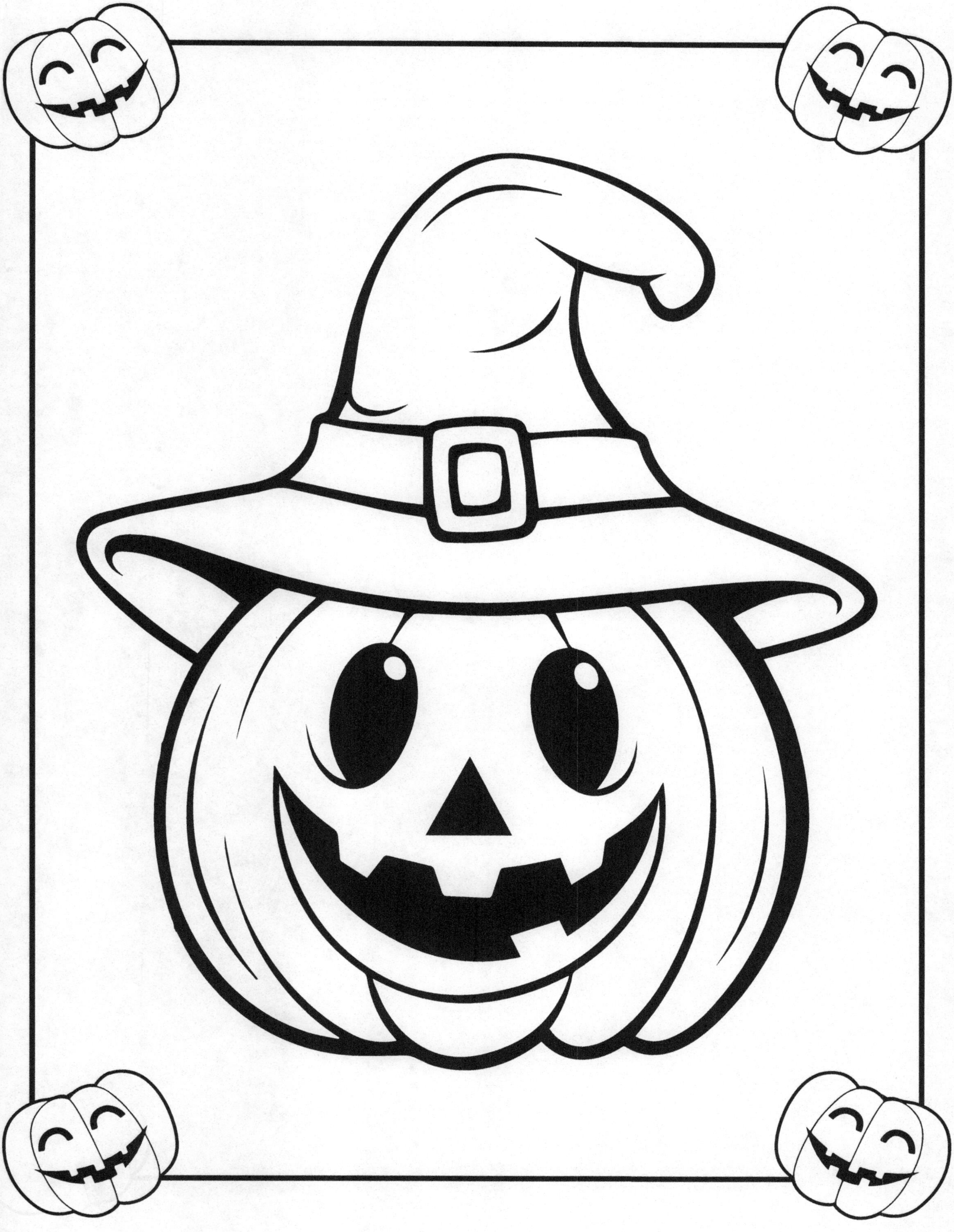

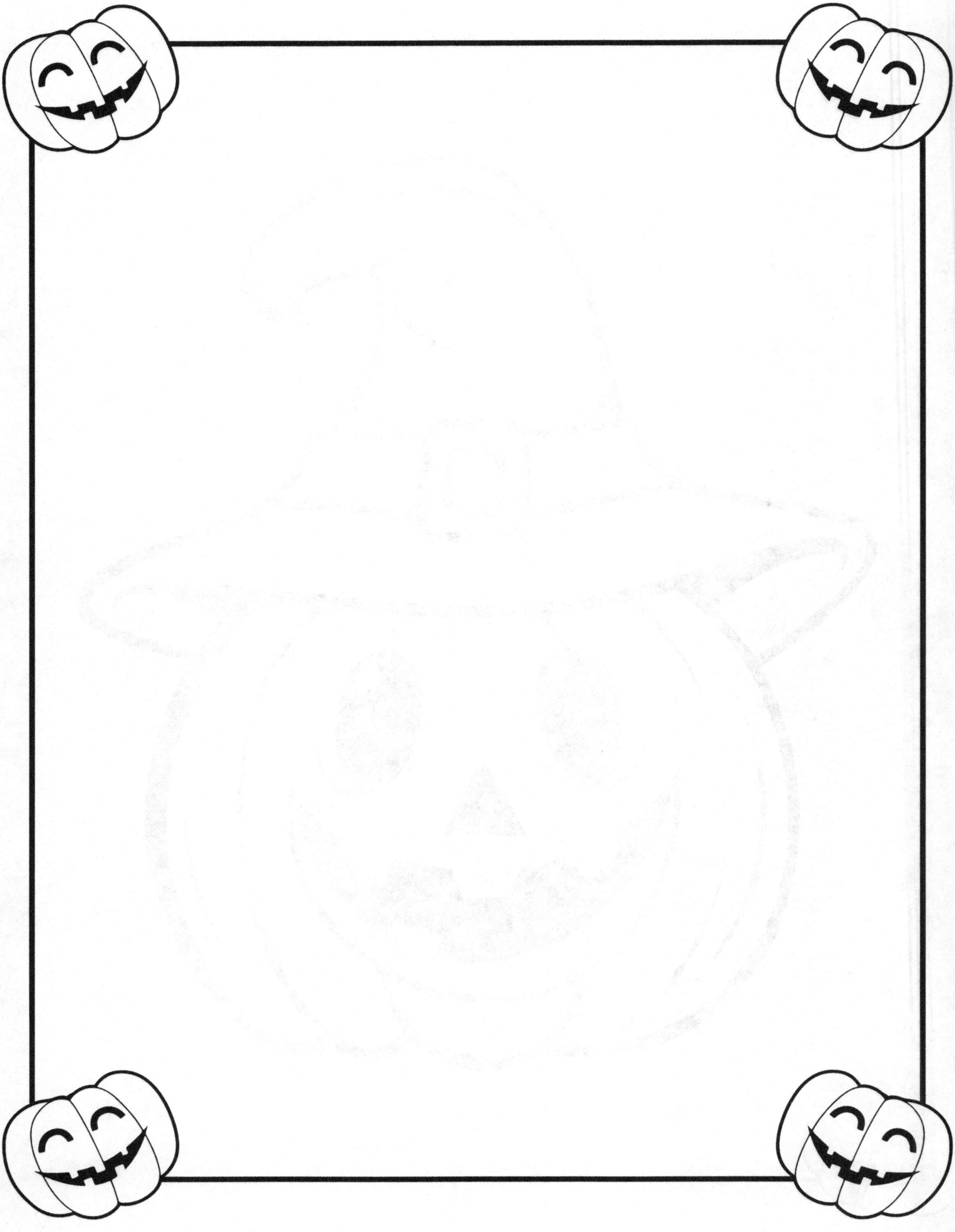

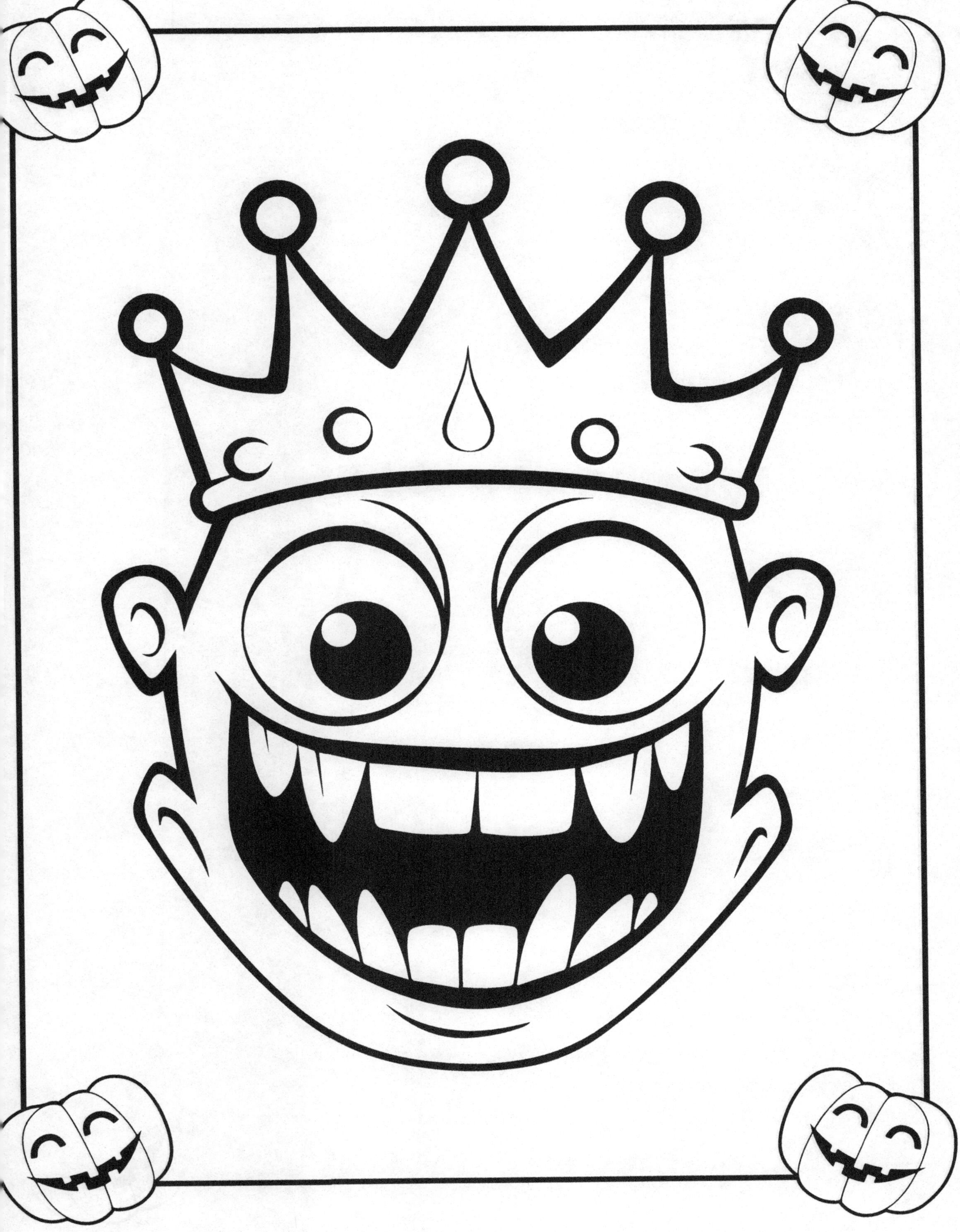

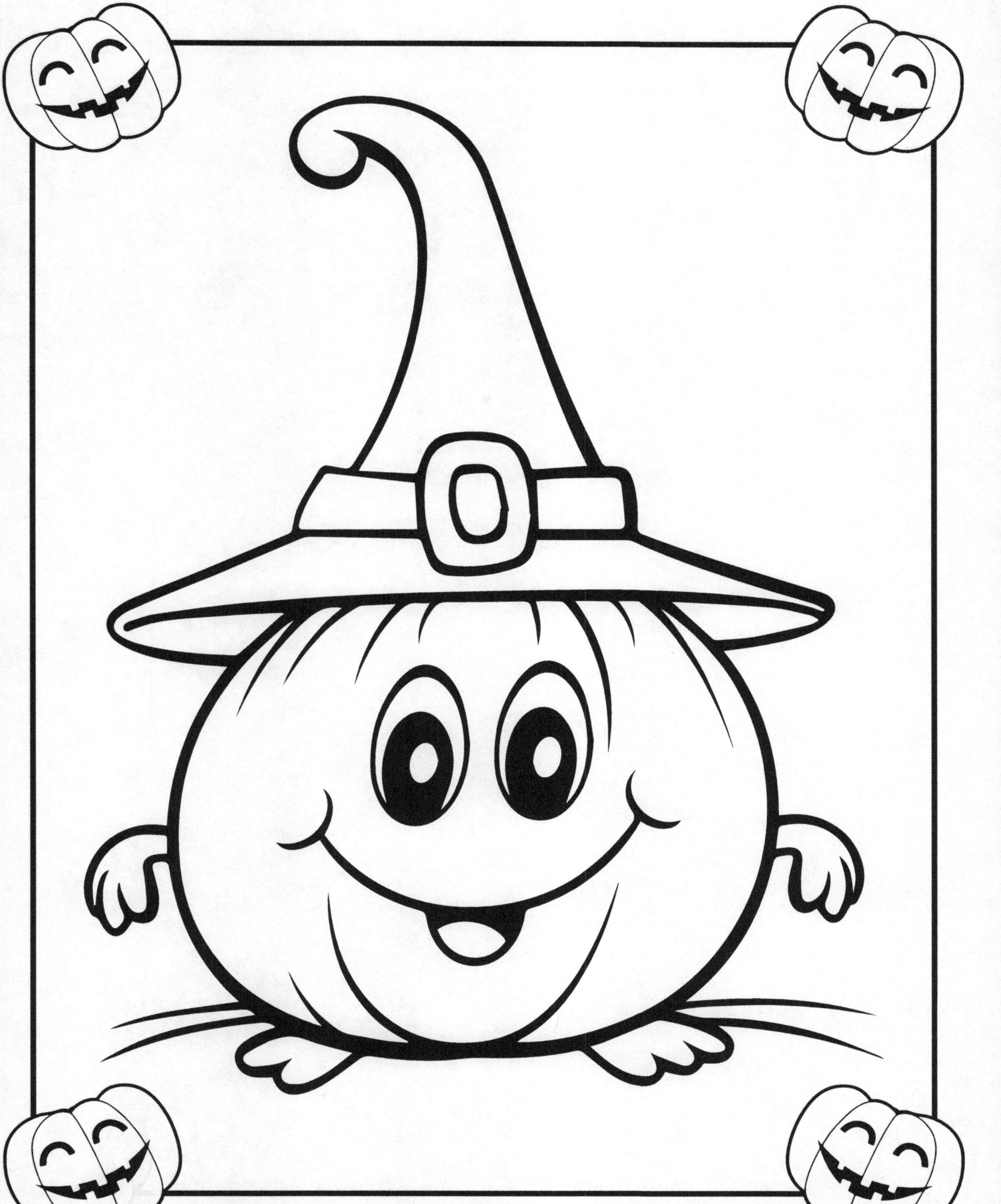

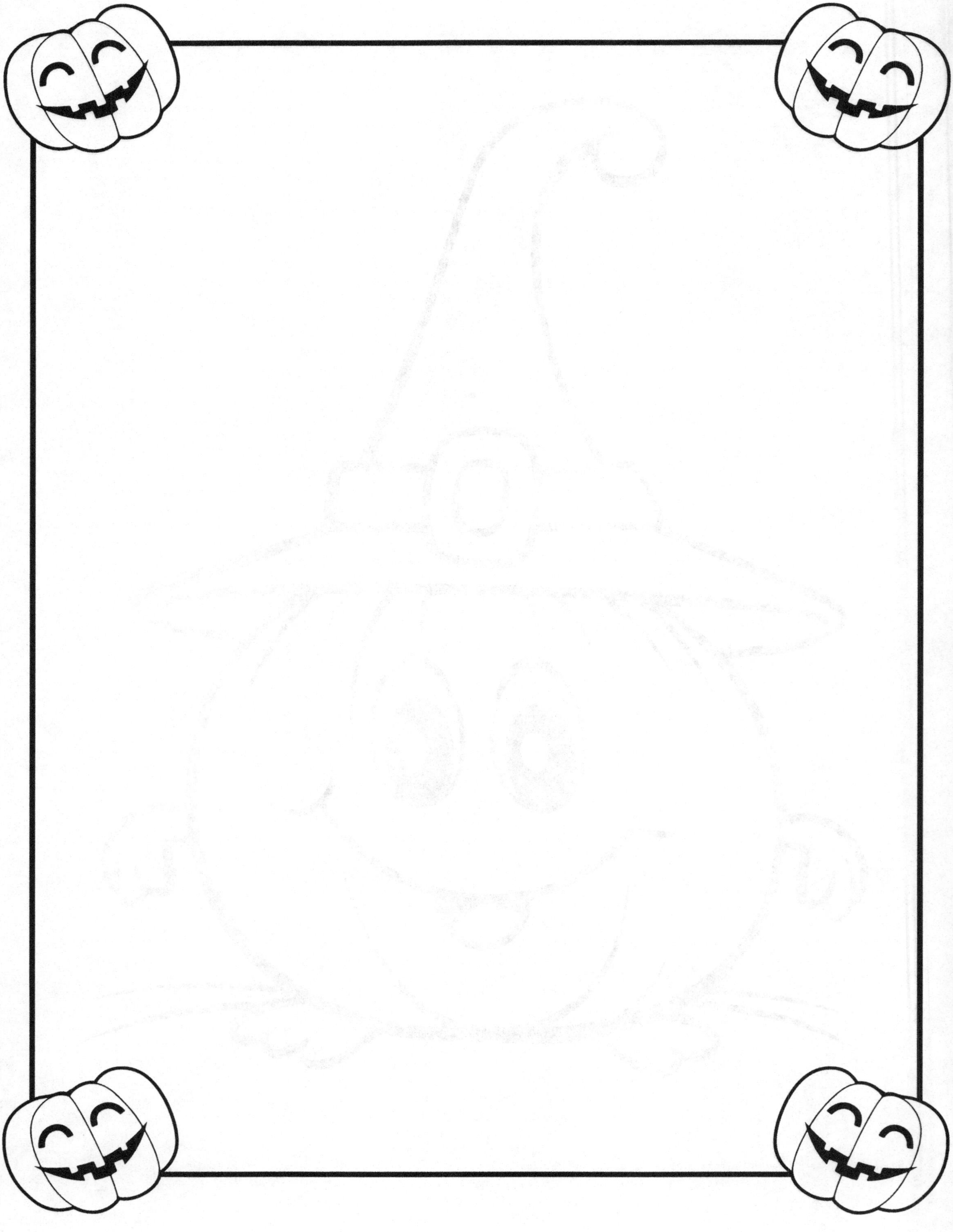

Made in the USA
Las Vegas, NV
08 October 2023

78796127R00059